FLUFFY TO COOKBOOK

SEASON everything with love

Notice

The outcome of a recipe depends on several factors such as ingredients, types of equipment, the reader's cooking ability, and judgement capabilities. Therefore, the author, editors, and publishers, do not take responsibility for the outcome of the recipes found in this book.

The reader must take the responsibility to review the listed ingredients before cooking to ensure none of the ingredients causes potential adverse effects to anyone consuming the food. Adverse effects include allergies and issues arising due to health-related restricted diet and/or pregnancy.

The dietary advice in this book is not meant as a substitute for any eating regimen that may have been prescribed by your doctor. As with all dietary programs, you should get your doctor's approval before beginning.

Mention of specific companies, organizations, or authorities in this book does not imply endorsement of the author, editors, or publishers.

Readers must take utmost safety measures when allowing children to cook in the kitchen. It is the reader's responsibility to supervise and assist the child all the time and ensure all necessary protection measures are taken. Monitor children if they are handling electrical appliances, and never allow children to handle sharp objects. Take extra care when children are working around hot surfaces. Teach children kitchen safety rules for a positive cooking experience.

The nutritional information provided for the recipes is estimated and for guidance only. I am not a dietician or medical professional. All the values provided are for the purpose of giving examples. Varying factors such as product type and brands purchased can change the nutritional values in any given recipe.

©2023 by Clare Morrow

All rights reserved. No part of this publication may be reproduced or transmitted in any form or by any means, electronic or mechanical, including photocopying, recording, or any other information storage and retrieval systems, without the prior written permission of the author.

Editors: Lacy Morrow M.A., Jennifer Weems

Front and back cover design by Cowgirl Creative

Photographer: Richard Martinez (front cover and inside portrait photos).

FLUFFY TO FIT COOKBOOK

CONTENTS

Acknowledgements---IV

Key---V

Introduction--- VII

How to Calculate your Calories and Macros-------------------1

How to Meal Prep--8

How to Maximize your Meals-------------------------------16

Cooking Tips--23

Breakfast--25

Lunch---32

Dinner--40

Midmorning Snacks--48

Afternoon Snacks---52

Salads--56

Sides---62

Sauces, Dips, and Dressings---------------------------------66

Desserts--72

Drinks and Smoothies---79

Acknowledgements

    I'd like to mention the following people for their contribution to the *Fluffy to Fit Cookbook*. Their invaluable time and energy made this book possible.

Thank you to my husband and workout partner Randy Morrow for his encouragement and input on this project. He was a taste tester for many of my recipes and a good sport about it too.

A special thanks goes out to my friend Jackie Boles for helping with food prep and design for the cover photo shoot.

Thank you to my editors Lacy Morrow, and Jennifer Weems, for working your magic of fine tuning all the details that bring a book to life.

Finally, a big thank you to all my wonderful followers on social media. Your words "Clare can you please do a cookbook?" sparked the idea for this project. I hope you enjoy it and find it useful for achieving your fat loss and fitness goals.

Key

 Denotes recipes that are beneficial to have one-hour pre or post workout because they contain a protein source and carbs. That combo promotes muscle growth and energy for working out.

 Denotes recipes that are good to have later in the day or as the last meal of the day because they do not contain carbs (particularly starchy kinds). These are meals that are easier to digest before going to sleep which promotes better results with fat loss.

 Denotes recipes that have a vegan version or vegan options for some of the ingredients.

* Meals are interchangeable. For example, you can make a lunch recipe for dinner or a breakfast recipe for your last meal of the day.

Follow me on my social platforms

@claremorrow_ifbbpro

| My Amazon Page | Instagram | Tik Tok | You Tube | Facebook | My Website |

In many of my recipes I use *Devotion* protein powder. *Devotion* is my go-to protein of choice for several reasons, it tastes great, contains quality whey protein isolate, micellar casein, and digestive enzymes. This is very important if you are lactose intolerant like I am. The digestive enzymes are what makes this protein stand apart. This is one of the only protein powders I can use without having stomach issues. It's also designed for baking so it's perfect for using in my recipes. If you use a different protein powder, I cannot guarantee that the flavor or texture of the food will be the same as what is shown in my recipes.

Shop Devotion at: Devotionnutrition.com (Use code: Clare10 for a discount).

Introduction

My first attempt at getting serious with my fitness journey began back in 2010 when I added a workout routine to my already busy life. The new workout plan helped me stay in decent shape, but because I made no real adjustments to my diet, I did not see the results I was hoping for. Once I learned the correct way of eating, along with addressing some hormone imbalances, I was finally able to lose fat and build muscle at the same time. Essentially, I began reshaping my body composition. The idea for this cookbook came from my experiences of what I did wrong and what I finally learned to do right. I hope it can be of help to anyone of any age who is looking to adjust their diet and get healthier.

Back when I first started working out, I was a professional equestrian with a busy routine. I spent my days training dressage horses and teaching riding lessons. My diet back then was a mixture of grabbing food on the go and meals out with my husband, Randy, or friends from the barn. Because I was active, I didn't worry much about what I ate. Did I eat like an a** hole most of the time? Yes, I did. So, it was no surprise that I was leaning towards the "fluffy" side of my ideal weight. I had no idea back then how to calculate macros and calories for my body type and activity level. It never occurred to me that drinking alcohol could stop fat loss for up to 24 hours. I would work out and then have some drinks on the weekends when we went out to dinner and then wonder why I wasn't seeing any changes with fat loss. In addition, my energy level wasn't 100 percent. There were many times where I would get busy and wait to eat until later in the day. I would be so hungry that I would just binge eat one big meal. Shortly after, I would feel like I needed a 2-hour nap! I'm so thankful I have learned how to shop for and prepare the right food, along with scheduling my meals to maximize my workouts, achieve fat loss, and not get that late-day food coma feeling. I'm excited to teach you how to achieve all of that in this book.

The reason I initially changed up my daily routine in 2010 was due to nagging shoulder pain that wouldn't go away. The doctor who examined me decided that I should get an MRI. From there, we discovered that the pain was coming from my neck. To my surprise, I had a herniated disc between C6 and C7. All those years of riding horses, especially the young ones, was taking a toll on my body. The doctor suggested I make an appointment with a rehabilitation therapist that could help me adjust some things to address the pain. I was surprised when the rehab therapist suggested I start doing some strength training to help build up my muscles around my neck. He felt like if I could build more upper body strength, it would help support my neck and spine better, and that could help take some of the stress off my neck and spine.

For two more years, I continued with the same routine. I was building up some decent muscle tone around my neck and shoulders which combined with other therapies to help ease my pain. Yet there wasn't much happening as far as noticeable change to my weight or the shape of my body. Looking back, it's no real surprise because I hadn't adjusted my diet at the time. In fact, during this time, Randy and I would often meet up at the gym to work out together and then we would celebrate our efforts by heading out to lunch at some "quasi healthy" chain restaurant. There we would indulge on rolls with butter, a salad (to try to stick with the "we are trying to be healthy" theme, while still pouring on the high calorie dressing). We would eat a main dish and then split a dessert to "not overdo it!" Yet really, we were eating back all the calories we had burned off at the gym. The liquid calories we consumed weren't helping either. Because I live in Texas, Dr. Pepper and sweet tea are often staple beverages for the southern palate. There we were stuck in the routine of eating whatever we felt like and working out a few times per week to try to ward off the "muffin middle" that eventually catches up with most of us as we age.

Real changes to mine and Randy's diets didn't happen until 2014. We were finishing up a session at the gym one day when I turned and saw a girl working out that had amazing muscle definition and a body shape that made me think *Wow! Okay how does that happen?* After she finished working out, I went up to talk to her about her routine. She informed me she was a bodybuilder, and she was getting ready to compete. I was intrigued. After we left the gym, I said to Randy, *Okay I have a new goal. I want to figure out what it takes to train and get in THAT kind of shape.* Never one to shy away from the crazy ideas of his red headed, energizer bunny, well-meaning, wife, Randy was all aboard. His reply was, *Clare, if bodybuilding is something you are interested in, let's do some research and find out more about it.*

With his wise words and encouragement, that's exactly what I did. I was 42 years old at that time. Within three years, at age 45, my hard work paid off, and I received my IFBB (International Federation of Bodybuilders) Pro card. If you are interested in learning more about mine and Randy's fitness journey, you can check out my book *Fluffy to Fit* which is available on Amazon. The book talks about everything we went through to get where we are today. It also has information on how to set up a workout plan, how to overcome gym shyness, the importance of hormone balance in relation to fat loss, and some great workout illustrations. The e-book version is also available at fluffytofitbook.com.

As I dove deeper into understanding what type of commitment it takes to become a bodybuilder, the biggest revelation was that losing fat and getting in shape wasn't going to happen from just working out. I finally had my "aha moment" when I learned that *fat loss is 80% diet*, and *you can't outrun your fork.*

I wrote this cookbook with a goal to help others achieve their fat loss and fitness goals with healthy, easy to follow, recipes. I've included a section on how to calculate your macros and calories and how to schedule the food you eat throughout the day to achieve fat loss (by being in a calorie deficit). It's also important to eat meals 3-5 times per day, so that you don't find yourself starving and then binge eating unhealthy food. Structuring your diet based on my recipes using whole, natural foods can give you back the energy you may have lost as you've gotten older. Many of my recipes also include good sources of protein, as well, which is important for building and maintaining muscles.

I've also included a short section on meal prep which gives you a better chance at being successful with your goals. It's important to be able to cook (or at least plan your diet correctly) when you get started adjusting what you eat. It's too easy to go off track if you eat out all the time, causing those unhealthy, high calorie foods, have a way of sneaking into our diets. In addition, cooking for yourself or your family, and meal prep, will be helpful when planning and sticking to your grocery budget.

If you love sweet stuff as much as I do, don't worry! I have included some tasty, low calorie dessert recipes, that allow you to stay on track with your weight goals while satisfying those sweet cravings too.

I turned 51 this year and Randy turned 69. We feel like we are in the best shape we can possibly be. We love sharing our journey that got us here with anyone who may need some direction or inspiration. I truly believe you are never too old to get in the best shape of your life. This book will help you learn how to maintain a diet plan that becomes a part of your healthy lifestyle. The alternative is usually a short-term *fad* diet, which people ultimately fail at because it doesn't set them up for long term success. My goal is to help you have the tools you need to succeed where you hadn't been able to before. So, with that…let's get cooking!

How to Calculate your Calories and Macros

Understanding your calories and macros is going to be important when choosing recipes that can help you achieve fat loss or maintain your goal weight. In addition, this information can be used to adjust the ingredients in the recipes if you need to swap some out. This happens occasionally due to budget, dietary reasons, or availability, since some ingredients can be seasonal. Once you have your calories and macros calculated out, it makes portioning out the correct amount of food for each of your meals very simple. All of that is helpful for being successful with your meal prep, which I cover in more detail in the meal prep section. The purpose behind my cookbook is to provide you with healthy, easy to follow recipes that help you formulate a meal plan that works in your favor for losing fat, building, and maintaining muscle, and creating a lifestyle of healthy eating. You can apply your macros and calories to your meal planning to customize what recipes work best for you.

Calories: Before we get into how to do the calculations for your daily caloric needs, it's important to understand what the heck calories are and why they matter. Calories are units of energy that a food or drink provides. We need calories to give us energy, to help us stay warm, and for healthy brain function. Not getting enough calories in our diet can lead to things like hair loss, fatigue, muscle loss, and even missed period cycles for women. Too many calories, especially from unhealthy sources, can lead to obesity, diabetes, heart problems, and can put strain and a lot more wear on our joints.

It may be obvious that fried, fatty, and processed foods tend to have more calories, while healthier foods, like fresh fruit and vegetables, tend to have less calories. However, it's important to note that some fruits and vegetables can be high in calories, while some things we consume, such as diet sodas, are low calorie, but they are mostly empty calories with no nutritional value. My recipes were created to take that into account. They contain vegetables that are better options to use when being in a calorie deficit and losing fat are part of your diet plan. Getting enough vegetables in as part of your daily diet is important because they are the best source for your micronutrients (i.e., vitamins and minerals). You just need to understand which ones are the better choices so that you stay within your caloric goals. That's what this cookbook is for: to help you see how planning ahead for different meals, while keeping in mind your goals, is the best way to stay on track for fat loss, weight maintenance, and overall better health.

A calorie calculator is a good resource because it takes into consideration your personal stats plus your weight goals and gives you a formula of how many calories you should be consuming in a day. I have a free calorie calculator on my website: claremorrow.com. A food tracking app, such as *My Fitness Pal,* is also a helpful when it comes to figuring out the nutritional value in foods or drinks and tracking what you eat during the day. Even though the recipes in this cookbook will have the calories and macros listed, it is always good to know how you can find the nutritional information for different foods if you swap out some of the ingredients in the recipes.

If you are not sure what "being in a calorie deficit" means and why it's important, briefly explained, it is the only way fat loss happens. A calorie deficit is when you consume less calories than you are burning off in a day. While there is no hard and fast rule when it comes to this, a 500-calorie deficit is usually an effective goal for weight loss. Essentially, if you are burning 2,500 calories per day, you would have a daily goal of consuming 2,000 calories per day.

One very important factor to keep in mind is that everyone's calorie intake is going to be different depending on their stats and goals. That's why I can't do anyone's personal calorie or macro calculations in this book, because I don't know your personal stats. When you calculate your calories, you will input your stats such as height, age, gender, activity level, and your weight goal. For example, you may want to maintain your current weight, aim for mild weight/fat loss, or go for extreme weight/fat loss. *Extreme fat or weight loss should be done under the supervision of a doctor. Entering your stats is so important because Kim who is 38 years old, 5' 3" tall, and works a desk job, will have much different caloric needs compared to Fiona who is 50 years old, 5' 9" tall, and has a very active job. Factors such as age, gender, lifestyle, and weight goals all play an important part of figuring out what your daily calories should be.

Being able to calculate your calories also enables you to adjust from being in a calorie deficit to maintenance calories, as needed. This is important to understand because a calorie deficit is not something that you need to be in all the time. Instead, it is a state you can be in when you need to lose fat and are trying to lean down. When you are in a calorie deficit you force your body to use nonfood sources for energy. Fat, for example, is a nonfood source. It will be burned off when you are in a calorie deficit, resulting in weight loss.

There really is no magic formula for how long you should be in a calorie deficit. Three months is usually the recommended time, but it can vary depending on your goals. Someone who is over 200 lbs., that is trying to lose 60 lbs. will be in a calorie deficit longer than someone who is 160 lbs. trying to lose 25 lbs. Typically the body will use fat (a nonfood source) at this stage in your diet. Calculating your caloric needs is important even if fat loss isn't a goal. It's important to get nutrients to maintain muscle and have plenty of energy to get through the day. Many people try to achieve fat loss by cutting out important nutrients, but that is not sustainable. My recipes are designed to show you that you can eat healthy, natural foods, that are satiating, while avoiding a VLCD (very low-calorie diet) which can lead to fatigue, hair loss, and nutritional deficiencies.

Macros: You may be wondering why we need to know what macros are and why the sources we get them from is important. "Macros" is short for macronutrients. Macros are made up of three categories of nutrients: protein, carbohydrates, and fat. Macros provide you with fuel for energy and the nutrients needed for building muscle and maintaining healthy brain function. Understanding macros and the best sources for them is important because it allows you to treat your body like a Ferrari. Not only do you need to know how much fuel is going in and out, but you want to know that your food (fuel for your body) is coming from a healthy source. Putting unhealthy food into your body is like putting bad fuel into the Ferrari. Do that a few times and not only will it run like crap, but it will also eventually break down. Unhealthy food for your body can have you feeling tired, possibly gaining weight, and probably will lead to health issues later in life.

Each of your macros has a specific number of calories. Calculating them is important because it helps to simplify choosing the types of macros you want for your meals. It can also make meal prepping easier, which I go over in more detail in the meal prep section.

Back to the Ferrari analogy. Unfortunately, our bodies do not have a gauge that shows "full" (like a car does) after we eat. The American diet, in general, has most people eating a lot more food than they need. Once you get stuck in that routine, it becomes hard to break the pattern, especially if most of what you are eating is calories from processed foods that are low on nutritional value. Food manufactures like to push those types of "foods" because they are rarely satiating and highly addictive, which gives them repeat customers, which leads to higher sales. You can see why that type of diet causes people to not know when their body has filled up on the correct amount of food, in relation to the energy they are expending that day.

That leads me to a great question I get asked a lot on my social platforms, "Clare, how do I know *how much* to eat in a day?" I like this question because it means that person has realized they've been eating like an a** hole. They've been getting by on processed foods, sodas, creamers and sugar in coffee, and over-processed bread and cheese, etc. Reality sets in when we realize we have no idea exactly what we should be eating, but we know that what we are eating isn't working. Figuring out the answer to that question can play a key part of successful fat loss and lead to a healthy diet for life.

Once I began to work with a bodybuilding coach and learned how important it was to not only eat the correct foods, but also keep track of exactly how much I was consuming and expending, I really saw changes happening. This was one of the motivating reasons behind coming out with this cookbook.

Doing the calculations for your macros and understanding the right kind of food you should be eating doesn't have to be overwhelming. I think a lot of people give up at this point because it either seems too complicated, or they think it will be a joy sucker. I have heard people say things like, "Ugh, calculating macros and calories? This is going to take all the fun out of eating." Or "Who cares? I'm not here for a long time, I'm just here for a good time." That's easy to say until you start having major health issues and then suddenly you are in some club you didn't sign up for.

Calculating your macros may seem tricky at first but it does get easier once you do it a few times. The first thing you will want to do is to locate a macro calculator to input your own stats. As I mentioned before, this is important since everybody is different and what works for you will not be the same as someone else. I have a free macro calculator located in the nav menu on my website, claremorrow.com.

Once you input your stats into the macro calculator you will get the amount in grams, of protein, carbs, and fat, you need in a day. You might also see the total calories you need for the day in the macro calculator. I prefer to use an actual calorie calculator for that since it is more accurate. You can use both calorie calculations if you want, just take the average from the two numbers you get. Once you know the number of macros that you need in a day, you will divide that out by the number of meals you usually have per day. I always recommend trying to get in at least three meals a day. If you can fit in 4-5 meals, even better. The meal prep section in this cookbook goes over how to portion your meals correctly for your calculations.

One easy rule of thumb to remember when it comes to macros and protein is that you should try for one gram of protein per pound of body weight, per day. So, if you weigh 140 lbs. try to get in 140 grams of protein per day. Correct protein intake is very important for building and maintaining muscle mass, especially as we age. If you are on the fluffier side (and I say that lovingly), for example you weigh 220 lbs. and your goal weight is 150 lbs., then go for your goal weight in grams of protein.

When it comes to calculating your macros, you will need to keep in mind that if you use a scoop of protein powder that has 20 grams of protein in it, then for one of your meals, let's say (as an example) that you had calculated your macros for four meals that day, you will want to drop down from 35 grams of protein to 15 grams for one of your meals because you got 20 grams of protein in from the powder. Or you can split it and drop two of your meals to 25 grams (deducting 10 grams of protein from each meal to equal the 20 g you got in from the protein powder). The same calculations would apply if you ate a bag of protein chips that day. If the chips had one gram of fat, six grams of carbs and 18 grams of protein, then you need to deduct those amounts from one of your meals later in the day.

It's important to note that you may need to revisit the macro and calorie calculators occasionally. Things like a difference in your daily activity level due to a career or lifestyle change, or if you hit a plateau with your fat loss, or you lose a significant amount of weight, can all be reasons why you would enter your stats again. When you first get started with fat loss, you won't want to change up your calorie intake too often. The same goes for your exercise routine. You need to give a new routine 2-3 months for results to show, otherwise you won't know what works and what doesn't.

I've included the macros and calories for each of my recipes which will make hitting your target goals a lot easier. Having healthy recipes to cook from plus knowing the macros and calories they contain can help you stay consistent with your diet. For optimal results, it's best to try to get in 4-5 smaller meals spread out through the day. You will want to try to eat your last meal of the day three hours before bedtime. This allows your body plenty of time to digest your food before you go to sleep.

Once you understand your macros and calories and have ideas of how to prepare tasty, healthy, low-calorie recipes that are still satiating, you will be much less likely to binge eat or go off track and just grab whatever food is available because that leads to choosing convenience over healthy, usually.

Remember to be patient with learning new recipes, especially ones that you prepare with your macro and calorie goals in mind. You should try to stick with your new cooking and meal prep routine for at least three months. Consistency is key to figuring out what works and what doesn't. Cooking healthy for yourself, and/or your family, can become an enjoyable part of your daily routine once you get the hang of it.

How to Meal Prep

In this cookbook, you will find many of my recipes that have helped me stay on track with my fat loss goals. Understanding how to incorporate meal prep into your routine will be helpful for cooking the recipes in larger amounts. Batch cooking is a great way to have healthy choices of food available at home and when you travel. Not having access to prepped food when you are out for the day or traveling leaves a lot of room for unhealthy food to sneak into your diet. Meal planning and prep is also a great way to form a grocery budget. When you know what to shop for each week and start buying food in bulk it really helps cut back on food expenses. Not to mention, eating out gets expensive and makes it easy to get off track when those buttered rolls hit the table, I don't know about you, but my willpower goes out the window faster than a teenager who gets a text at night from her boyfriend! If you feel pressed for time and think meal prep will be hard to fit into your schedule, you would be surprised that my easy-to-follow recipes only take a few hours to make and then you can have all your meals ready for the week.

Before I go over how to portion food for prep, I wanted to list a few items I have found to be helpful with cooking and storing food. I have most of these listed on my *Amazon* page under "Kitchen Favorites" and "Food Swaps." Located at: claremorrow.com/amazon-favorites.

1. Crockpot: A crockpot doesn't have to be fancy or expensive to be useful. Crockpots come in handy for cooking food in bulk. I use mine to cook chicken breasts (white meat is a less fatty choice) in the crockpot, where they simmer for several hours in their own juices. You can also cook meat balls in bulk and let them simmer in red sauce for a few hours. Those are just a few

examples of how you can batch cook healthy food. I go over more examples in my recipes. Yes, you can use a large saucepan to cook in bulk, but this requires monitoring the food while it's cooking and breaking out a sauce pan usually has us adding some type of cooking oil, so food doesn't stick. Calories from unmeasured amounts of oil will add up fast. The nice part about the crock pot is it allows food to cook in its own juices or you can add a little water.

2. Air fryer: I can't live without that sucker! I use it to cook everything from fish to sweet potatoes. I even use it to make cloud bread pizza. The recipe for Cloud Bread is included in this cookbook because it's a great low-calorie bread substitute. It can be used to make wraps, pizza, and other healthy, great tasting, recipes.

3. Food Scale: This is a necessity for meal prep so you can weigh out the portions that you dish out into your meal prep containers. I like to use a digital scale because it helps me be precise. Once you have your macros calculated, you will understand how many grams of each of your protein, carbs, fat, you need for the day. For prepping, you simply divide that out by how many meals you are planning for the day. I try to get in 4-5 meals per day since it allows me to eat smaller meals throughout the day, while still getting in my macros. This also makes it easier to pack meals on the go. One thing to note is that you can weigh your food raw or cooked. Just make sure that you enter it that way in your food tracking app.

4. Meal Prep Containers: There are a ton of varieties available when it comes to containers. I have some of my favorites listed on my Amazon page. You can choose the ones that fit your fridge storage space best. Having easy-to-use prep containers on hand makes portioning and storing food so much easier. It is also helpful to use them when traveling, so they are worth having.

5. Sugar Free Sauces: When I go live on my social media pages and show meal prep, one comment that comes up often is "Clare, you don't use seasoning?" When it comes to seasoning, I like to

do things differently. Since I am cooking in bulk for meal prep, rather than using the same one or two seasonings where the food tastes the same after a while, I wait to add flavor in the form of different sauces when I am heating up my meals. This is my secret to never having boring food, even though my basic recipe stays the same. My favorite sauces are the *G. Hughes* brand. They are sugar free, which means low calorie, but they are super flavorful and there's a variety to choose from. These are also located on my *Amazon* page under my food swap list.

Now that you have a better idea of some benefits of meal prep plus a few of my favorite products that can help make it easier, here is an example of how-to meal prep by cooking and then portioning out your macros for the day. **Remember this is just an example. You should use a macro calculator to figure out your macros for your own stats. There is a free calculator on my website: claremorrow.com.**

My example meal prep is for *Julie*. She has done the calculations for both her macros and calories for her stats. Julie needs 140 grams of protein, 200 grams of carbs, and 60 grams of fat, per day. Her total calories for the day are 1860. Julie has used a food tracking app to figure out how many calories are in of the different macros she is choosing as food sources for her meal prep. (I will have calories and macros listed in each of my recipes for an understanding of what that looks like).

The next step for Julie is to divide the total daily grams for each macro by the number of meals she is planning on having for the day. For this example, I am using four meals. Using her macro calculations from above, 140 grams of protein divided by four meals, means Julie needs 35 grams of protein for each meal. For her carbs she is going to divide 200 grams by four, which equals 50 grams of carbs for each meal. For fat (make sure it's from a healthy source), she needs 15 grams with each meal. Julie's total calories for the day are 1,860. Divide that by four meals and each meal (composed of her macros) should equal 462 calories per meal. You might have noticed that I did not include vegetables in the basic calculations. Veggies and fruits are considered micronutrients (not macros). Although you will hear me say, "There are no bad veggies," I recommend trying to stick with ones that that have less carbs/natural sugars. Broccoli, asparagus, cauliflower, and green beans are good choices. Some veggies, like carrots, sweet peas, and corn, have more carbs/natural sugar. I'm not saying to never have those, just be mindful of veggie choices when fat loss is a goal. You can add as many healthier choices of veggies as you want to each meal or save them to have as a late day meal or snack.

When it comes to fruit in your diet, berries will be your best choice. They have less sugar than others such as apples, pineapple, watermelon, and bananas. Choosing fruit, like blueberries, strawberries, raspberries, and blackberries, will still allow you to get the beneficial vitamins and minerals in your diet, without adding a lot more calories from the natural sugar found in fruit. You will want to count the calories from veggies and fruit in your food tracking app as well since they do count as part of your daily total calories. Fruit can be mixed in with your oats in the morning or be added to a protein smoothie in between meals. I like to get my fruit in earlier in the day (usually pre-workout) since it enables my body to process the fructose better while I'm more active during the day. Eating fruit late at night may cause your body to store the fructose as fat instead.

There will be times where you will have to adjust your meal prep and portions. If you eat breakfast at home, then you might only need to prep three or four meals. Remember though, you would subtract the calories and macros your breakfast contains from your totals for the day. The rest would be split between the meals you prep. The benefits of understanding your macros and calories for the day are that it makes it so much easier to adjust and still stay on track if you will be away from home. For example, if you have a busy week coming up where you will be away from home, you can prep five meals for each day of the week. Pack up three with you and have two at home for the early morning and your last meal of the day. Try to eat your last meal at least three hours before bedtime so your body has time to digest the food.

When it comes to portioning out food for your meal prep, I've created an example using one of my basic recipes. **The portions are based on the example calculations above.** First, I take some chicken breasts and put them in the crock pot to slow cook. They are the protein portion of the meal. (You can sub out for another lean meat of choice or a vegan option). Next, I take three or four sweet potatoes, or Japanese yams, slice them up, and put them in the air fryer. This is going to be the carbs. Then, I take a vegetable like broccoli and steam it. Once the chicken is cooked, I place it on paper towels to drain. Next, I take one of my meal prep containers and place it on the digital scale and then I tare the scale. (This sets it to zero, so my container weight does not count as part of my macros). I like to weigh my food after it is cooked, but you can weigh your food raw or cooked, just make sure you enter it in the app that way when calculating your macros. Next, I use metal tongs to pick up some of the chicken and place the chicken in the container that is on the scale. I weigh the chicken (in grams), adding or removing as needed to get the correct amount which is 35 g protein per meal. This is based on my example calculations (140 g protein per day). I repeat this step with my carbs. I tare the scale again to zero, I take a few of the cooked sweet potatoes and place them in the container on the scale. My carb portion needs to be 60 grams for each meal. (200 g per day). After my protein and carbs are weighed and portioned, I fill up the rest of my meal prep containers with the broccoli. I repeat weighing and portioning my food until I fill up 14 containers with the chicken and potatoes and some veggies or a salad. That gives me two meals per day that are prepped.

For my next recipe to prep for meal three, I might boil some peeled shrimp (frozen or fresh), which are a healthy source of protein that is lower in fat. Next, I'll make up a large batch of jasmine rice (my carb), and I'll prep a large salad. For dressing, I like to make my own and store it separately. I don't like to pour it on the salad because it tends to get soggy, and I have no idea of the amount I'm using. For healthier dressing that enables me to get in some of my daily fat content, I mix MCT oil (from coconuts or palm kernels) with a little vinegar and lemon juice. I put my dressing in a spray bottle to lightly spray on my salad when it's plated. For a more flavorful dressing, you can mix a ranch seasoning pack with some Greek yogurt. I have some good dressing recipes in the salads section. Next, I repeat the steps of placing the container on the scale, tare it to zero, weigh out 35 g of shrimp, 60 g of rice, and add some cooked veggies or the salad. I'll make seven of these meals, so now I have 21 meals prepped and am set for the week.

In the example meal prep, I showed how to cook your protein and carbs. Fat is also one of your macros. You will want to get some fat into your diet, remember though, *we don't need to eat a lot of fat to lose fat*. I try to meet my daily fat requirement from my meat (protein) choices. If needed, you can add healthy sources of fat to your meals: you could cook with a measured amount of MCT Oil, add olives or avocado to your salad, and even cook salmon on occasion. (I try to stick with white fish as much as possible since it has less fat). In small amounts, those are sources of healthy fat that you can use to meet your daily needs.

If you are prepping your breakfast, you can include things like egg whites (which have less fat if you are trying to stay in a calorie deficit), boiled whole eggs (higher in fat so be careful of too many whole eggs), steel cut oats, fresh or frozen berries, Greek yogurt, and protein waffles with a little sugar free maple syrup on the side to dip them in, are all easy to prep breakfast ideas. I have a whole section on healthy, low calorie, breakfast recipes later in the book. Because I work out early in the day, I try to make sure I get some protein and a good amount of carbs in before my workout. This is important for having fuel in my body, so I have energy. I talk more about this in the section "How to Maximize your Meals."

When it comes to dessert and snacks, I usually do not add these to my prepped meals. Instead, I will either make a protein smoothie to have in between my meals, or make a dessert with protein, like my chocolate protein dipping sauce and strawberries. I might have a rice cake with some chocolate protein sauce and peanut butter powder mixed with water on top. PB2 is good, and it's a low-calorie option. I have this also on my *Amazon* page under "Food Swaps." I try to limit using smoothies as a meal replacement because there are benefits to chewing food. When we chew our mouth releases saliva that aids in digestion. In addition, the act of chewing has our body releasing our satiating hormones that let us know when we are full. Protein smoothies come in handy for in between meals and can be helpful for getting in more protein for the day. I use *Devotion Protein* for smoothies, and I also use it to make some great tasting desserts that are healthier options. These are healthier choices that can help me get in some of my macros while also satisfying my sweet cravings. I will go over this in more detail in my dessert section.

Keep in mind, macros and calories from smoothies or any snacks will count towards your daily totals. That is why even if you do meal prepping, you still want to enter everything you eat and drink into your food tracking app. If you end up having one black coffee during the day and put a scoop of protein powder in it, that's 20 grams, and then if you eat a rice cake with protein powder mix on it, that's another 20 grams of protein. So, one of your prepped meals would need to have 40 grams less protein. The same goes with any in between meal snacks that have carbs. So, if your prepped meal for dinner already has chicken for your protein and potatoes for your carbs, you may need to remove some of that to get your number on track for the day. You can do the reverse and use protein powder to get in more for the day if your meals do not have quite enough.

If you are on a vegan or plant-based diet, you will need to make sure you get enough protein from other sources that can provide you with some healthy fats. Many times, a vegan diet requires BCAA supplements.

These are important amino acids that come mostly from meat protein. It's always best to check with a doctor about any supplements you might need if you think you are deficient.

Cooking and prepping the recipes in this book can help you stay in a calorie deficit if you are trying to lean down and stay at your maintenance calories in between. If you have tried to stick to a healthy diet before and didn't have success, incorporating meal prep into your daily routine might help you this time around. I also have some meal prep videos on my *YouTube* channel that you might find helpful.

How to Maximize Your Meals

The goal of my cookbook is to provide you with great tasting, easy to follow recipes, that allow you to structure your diet according to your calculated macros and calories. Even if fat loss isn't your goal and you are just trying to maintain your weight, it's important to make sure you get in enough calories from the right kinds of food. A common mistake people make when it comes to fat loss is thinking that eating one meal per day is a healthy way to lose weight. Or they try to substitute meals with a smoothie thinking liquid as a dietary source will prevent them from gaining weight. The problem is when you withhold food from your body for too long, you risk getting *hangry*. That can lead to binge eating. The next thing that happens is a detour through *Cluck-in-a-Bucket* drive through simply because it's convenient, and you need food "now." When this happens, you may be tempted to punish yourself the next day by making yourself do extra cardio or even skipping a meal. While you may think that is helpful it's not a good idea. If you do find yourself going off on a binge fest with a cheat meal, or even a cheat day, don't punish yourself. Just drink a lot of water to flush your system and then get back on track with your diet and workouts as soon as you can. Eating correctly and consistently is how you build a lifestyle of healthy eating, but it can take up to several months for that routine to really stick.

Maximizing your meals means planning your diet (eating schedule) in a way that benefits your energy level, keeps you satiated throughout the day, and helps you maintain good digestive health. This allows you to utilize your calories in a way to achieve fat loss, build muscle, and have more energy throughout the day. If you have been eating irregularly, even though you have cut back on calories, you may see some fat loss initially, but you will probably hit a plateau after a short while and you may find yourself lacking energy to get through your day.

Through my "fluffy to fit" journey, including becoming a competitive bodybuilder, I've learned how to plan my meals so that I can use what I eat to help me with fat loss while building muscle to reshape my body. It also helps me keep my energy level consistent. As we age, eating correctly is particularly important because our digestion tends to slow down due to us not being as active. I'm sure I'm not alone when I say I just can't eat a lot of the foods I could when I was in my 20s and even 30s. When it comes to eating a lot of starchy carbs late in the day or too much dairy, which is so overprocessed these days, my body lets me know it. *Hello! Bloated toad party of one*! Working out regularly not only helps with fat loss and building muscle to support our bones, but movement in general can help aid our digestion. Plus, exercising daily can help us build up a thirst which means we are likely to drink more water. I always recommend trying to get in one gallon of water per day because there's so many benefits to staying well hydrated.

I've listed a few of the ways you can *Maximize Your Meals* below:

1. If fat loss is a goal, try fasted cardio. This means you wake up and have black coffee only, then do your cardio for 20 minutes. I like to do mine on speed three, incline eight. If you hit a plateau with fat loss, you can adjust the incline to be higher (for a while), which will increase the intensity and you will burn more calories. You can do your cardio on any machine you prefer. The main idea for fasted cardio is to get your heart rate to 130-140 bpm (beats per minute). Fasted cardio is also a good option if you're tight on time since it saves you from having to prepare, eat, and digest a meal before exercising. It's also an effective option if you have a sensitive stomach or feel more energetic without a meal before a workout. When it comes to lifting and workouts, you DO NOT want to do those fasted. We need food as fuel to have the

strength to workout. Lifting fasted can be dangerous since you could become lightheaded and drop the weights causing injury. Once I am done with fasted cardio, I make sure to fuel up with a meal that has protein and carbs from healthy sources, which helps with recovery.

2. Eating a balanced meal that has enough protein and carbs one hour before lifting (strength training) is a beneficial way to fuel up your body for energy and building muscle. I like to eat one hour before my work out and about one hour after. I have recipes of my favorite pre and post workout meals in the recipe section. Did you know that our bodies continue to burn calories for up to 48 hours post lifting? That's because muscle mass is built by small micro tears that happen in our muscle tissue when we lift. This is also why you will feel sore after lifting. As the muscle tissue heals, it also grows. Because muscle growth is a continual process, I make sure to keep my protein intake consistent throughout the day, even on my days off from working out. Fat loss from calories being burned during the muscle growth stage happens on rest days too.

3. When it comes to eating protein or carbs, it's recommended to get both in your meals. For example if you have a ground turkey burger, have some sweet potatoes on the side. If you are having a vegan protein like lentils or quinoa, have it with some rice. The carb portion of your meal provides you with energy, while the protein portion helps build muscle. The two work well together to keep your body healthy and functioning.

4. Intermittent fasting is a new trend that I get asked about a lot when I go live on my social pages. "Clare, what about intermittent fasting?" My answer is always the same. I do not do it or recommend it for the reasons stated above in section number two. If you are working on fat loss, and building muscle at the same time, whether it's to reshape your body, to compete, or just to fill out loose skin, your body needs to be fed good sources of protein to repair and grow

muscle. In addition, intermittent fasting leaves us more susceptible to binge eating. We might have good intentions to withhold food for 14 hours and then someone walks into the room with a box of donuts and its game over! Healthy carbs on a consistent basis are going to be helpful for brain function, proper digestion, regulation of our blood cholesterol, and strength when lifting.

5. Coffee or tea in the morning is fine. As I mentioned before, fasted cardio is a great way to burn calories for fat loss. You don't want to add anything to your coffee or tea otherwise it's not truly being in a fasted state. Before you jump (or crawl for some of us) out of bed and head to the kitchen in the morning, try to just drink water for the first 10 minutes after getting up. You want to let your cortisol levels (our waking up hormone) get going as naturally as possible. Our cortisol levels will naturally elevate in the morning because we are exiting our sleep stage. As we wake and get moving around, our cortisol will start to do its job and our energy level will increase. If you can allow your body a little time to adjust and just have water to hydrate your organs, and then hit the coffee or tea, it can be helpful for keeping your cortisol hormone working the way it should. You can also have coffee or tea later in the day. Either for more energy or to help curb a sugar craving. Instead of refined sugars, try adding some cinnamon to your coffee of tea instead. If you need sweetener, try Monk Fruit Sugar or Stevia (both are on my *Amazon* page under my "Food Swap" lists). Be careful of adding unmeasured amounts of cream to your coffee or tea. The calories from that can add up at the end of the day. If you do add any cream or sugar to drinks, you will want to add that in your food tracking app. You can include your coffee or tea as well even though the calories are minimal. When tracking your food, it's always a good idea to include everything you put in your mouth if you really want to

be accurate. I also have a recipe in this book for a protein-based frothy foam to add to coffee. It's a tasty, low-calorie way to jazz up your coffee and get in some extra protein for the day.

6. Let's talk fruit. I mentioned in the previous section how fruit along with veggies is the best source of micronutrients. When it comes to fruit, I try to stick with the berries since they have the lower amounts of natural sugars. I'm not saying to never have pineapple, watermelon, bananas, or oranges. I'm just saying to be careful of them if fat loss is one of your goals. I like to eat my fruit earlier in the day when I'm more active because it allows my body to digest the carbs/natural sugars better. I try to get my fruit in pre-workout, mixed in with my oatmeal, or I will add some to a *Devotion* protein smoothie post-workout in between my meals, earlier in the day. I also want to talk about fruit juice. For the most part, it is not a good idea to drink it. Most fruit juices, yes even orange juice, are loaded with sugar. It's best to eat your fruit in its natural form. If it grows on a bush or a vine, it's usually fine.

7. When it comes to carbs, especially starchy carbs like potatoes, rice, pasta, I try to not overdo them late in the day. Part of maximizing my meals is getting them in before 3:00 pm. This will work best if you plan on doing fasted cardio in the morning. You don't want to go to bed with a belly full of pasta or rice and have glycogen floating around your body if you are trying to release fat stores with your fasted cardio. In addition, if you have ever had days where you get busy and don't have time to eat until late in the afternoon and you eat a big meal with a lot of carbs, then the next thing you know it's 3:00 pm, and you feel like taking a two-hour nap and you're not sure how you will get through the rest of the day. That's what I like to call the *food coma effect*. To avoid that, try getting in most of your carbs earlier throughout the day (based on the calculations for your macros). Getting your carbs in earlier in the day can help prevent that late day energy crash.

8. Protein is one of the most important macros that aid your body in building muscle. Whether your protein is from meat or vegan sources, make sure you try to get in your daily requirement from healthy foods. A general rule of thumb is one gram of protein per pound of body weight per day. If you weigh 155 pounds, then you will need 155 grams of protein per day. Split that up equally between your 3-5 meals per day. If you are on the *fluffier* side and trying to slim down, go for your goal weight in protein. If you find it difficult on some days to get enough protein, then you can supplement it with a good protein powder like *Devotion*. You can also make dessert using it. I have some great recipe examples in the dessert section. There are also protein snacks you can choose if you don't have time to get all your protein in from your meals. I have some protein snacks I like on my *Amazon* page under my "Food Swaps" list.

9. When it comes to getting in your veggies, it's fine to eat them throughout the day, or you can save up most of them for later in the day. I try to get in my last meal three hours before bedtime. This schedule allows my food to have a chance to digest before I go to sleep. I know it's not always possible to schedule our meals like this because we all get busy. If you get most of your meals in earlier in the day and you feel hungry right before bedtime, I have some ideas for early evening snacks that are healthier option in the recipes section.

10. Let's talk about sugar. Did you know that we do not need ANY added sugar in our diets? Yet, the average person living in the U.S. consumes around 70 grams per day. I have a whole chapter in my book *Fluffy to Fit* on how to beat sugar cravings because it's a problem for so many people. Food manufacturing companies love sugar. It's cheap, easy to come by, and highly addictive. They add it to everything they can to get repeat customers that can never get enough. I know it's a hard habit to break, but it is possible. You just need to start cutting back to smaller and smaller amounts and use replacements, like cinnamon in your coffee or on your

oats. Use healthier plant-based sugar replacements like Monk Fruit sugar to try to cut back on refined sugar when you can. If you can't completely cut out added sugar, try to make sure to not have more than 25 grams per day (for women) and 35 grams per day for men.

The next section of the book contains some of my favorite recipes I have found to be helpful for me to be successful on my fitness journey. Randy and I love food just as much as the next person. It took us a few years to learn how to eat correctly so that we still get to enjoy great tasting food, while being able to lose fat, build muscle, and become our healthiest versions of ourselves. This cookbook gives us an opportunity to pass on what we have learned. Our fitness journey has evolved to not only being able to help ourselves feel great but being able to inspire others to do the same. We hope you find this cookbook helpful and will use it as a guide on your journey to look and feel your very best.

Cooking Tips

1. In many of my recipes I use *Devotion* protein, my protein powder of choice. It not only tastes great, but it also contains quality whey protein isolate, micellar casein, and digestive enzymes. This is very important if you are lactose intolerant like I am. The digestive enzymes are what makes this protein stand apart. I can use it without having stomach issues. It's also designed for baking so it's perfect for using in my recipes. If you have dairy allergies or follow a vegan diet, you can substitute it with vegan protein. Try to find one that is suitable for baking. **If you use a different protein powder, I cannot guarantee that the flavor or texture of the food will be the same as what is shown in my recipes.**

2. Adjusting recipes to make them your own is what makes cooking fun and brings a personal touch to finished dishes. If necessary, you might find you need to switch out some ingredients for any number of reasons. It could be that some foods are seasonal, or you might start a recipe and not have all the ingredients on hand. If you follow a vegan diet, you might need to swap out some of the non-vegan foods. Feel free to take any of the recipes in my book and adjust them to what works for you. Two things to keep in mind are that you will need to adjust the macros for any changes to ingredients or portion sizes, and I cannot guarantee how the flavor or consistency will be if you do make changes.

3. When you cook, there are factors, other than the ingredients you use, that can change how food cooks and tastes. Some examples are cooking with gas vs. cooking with electricity, the mineral content in the water you use, the types of pots or pans you use (e.g., dark coated vs. noncoated), and the quality of cookware, such as blenders and mixers. Finally, you must consider how you measure your ingredients. Some people feel comfortable not measuring and they cook from their heart. Others must measure everything twice. All those things can make recipes vary, but that's what makes cooking a fun and rewarding challenge.

4. When fat loss is a goal, every calorie counts. You will see that most of my recipes say to use nonstick cooking spray instead or cooking oil. That's because the calories from unmeasured amounts of cooking oil add up fast! So, while it may be tempting to dump a few Tbs of olive oil in the pan, keep in mind there's a reason I do not have that listed as a step for many of the recipes in my cookbook.

5. It's important to get some fruits and vegetables in our diet every day. Not only are they a healthy source of vitamins and minerals, but most also have less calories and fat compared to other processed foods. You will find throughout my recipes that I stick to certain fruits and veggies. That's because some are lower in natural sugar and calories. Berries are my favorite choice for fruit. Blueberries, strawberries, and raspberries are a great source of micronutrients with less fat, calories, and added sugar than others. Some examples of fruit that I stay away from daily are pineapple, watermelon, and bananas. I use those as ingredients in recipes that I

make as an occasional dessert. When it comes to veggies, I stick to the green ones such as broccoli, spinach, green beans, asparagus, and cucumber. The ones I have occasionally are carrots, peas, and beets. If you are not sure which fruits and veggies are the best to choose from, you can use a food tracking app like *My Fitness Pal* to check and compare the macros before deciding which ones to use if you need to sub out some of the ingredients in the recipes.

6. Let's talk about nuts. Several of my recipes include nuts. You will see that it is mainly slivered almonds. Yes, nuts are a healthy source of fats, but be careful of having too many of them when fat loss is a goal. Some nuts are higher in fat and calories than others. Use your food tracking app to check the macros of each kind before throwing a handful of walnuts on your recipe. You would be surprised that nuts can increase the macros by 100 calories or more! So, just don't go nuts with your nuts. Lol!

7. Meal Prep 101: Having the correct cooking utensils and good containers to store your food in for the week makes cooking that much more enjoyable. There's nothing more of a beating than when you get all done cooking a large batch of food and now you must rummage around the kitchen to find containers to put it in and pray that at least some of the lids (of the 1200 random ones that have mysteriously multiplied at night) will fit. Lol! Being organized in the kitchen ahead of cooking and meal prep makes the whole process much more enjoyable.

8. Invest in a food scale. Not only does it come in handy for measuring out ingredients, it's also the best way to be accurate with portioning your food for meal prep. I have a scale that I like listed in my *Amazon* store.

9. Ovens can lie. Lol! Don't rely solely on the cooking time listed in the recipes. Use your smell, taste, and the good old "toothpick in the middle" test, to check if food is done. Use a meat thermometer when baking or grilling meat to ensure it is fully cooked.

10. Always taste your food before seasoning it. I prefer to leave off the seasoning when I cook chicken and fish. I cook most of my food in bulk, so I can meal prep for the week. Instead of having all the food seasoned and tasting the same, I leave off the seasoning and add different flavored sauces to each meal before I have it. I use the *G Hughes* sugar free sauces since they taste great, and I can add variety in flavor to the food I cook in bulk.

11. Clean as you go. If the thought of cleaning a giant mess prevents you from enjoying the benefits of cooking and meal prep, try cleaning as you go. It makes a huge difference.

12. Use parchment paper to line pans as much as possible when cooking. It helps immensely with not having to wash your pans afterward.

BREAKFAST RECIPE 1 ⭐

Egg White Omelette

PREP TIME: 10 MINUTES

COOK TIME: 10 MINUTES

READ IN: 20 MINUTES

INGREDIENTS

- 4 LARGE EGG WHITES
- ¼ TSP KOSHER SALT
- 1/3 TSP FRESHLY GROUND BLACK PEPPER
- 1 TBS GRATED PARMESAN CHEESE*
- ¼ CUP CHOPPED SCALLION, GREEN PART
- 1/3 CUP FIRM CHERRY TOMATOES HALVED

For added flavor, serve with my low-calorie salsa. Recipe can be found on the sauces page.

SERVINGS: 1 OMELETTE

MACROS: 4g CARBS, 19g PROTEIN, 2g FAT, 3g SUGAR

CALORIES: 149 CALORIES

NOTES: *Eggs are nutrient rich and provide quality protein. They are a healthy source of vitamin A and D. When fat loss is a goal, egg whites are a good substitute because the yolk is higher in fat. A good ratio is to have three egg whites and one whole egg per day as part of your diet. This allows you to get the health benefits of eggs while being mindful of calories.*

STEPS

1. Heat a nonstick 8-inch skillet over medium heat for one to two minutes.
2. Meanwhile, in a medium bowl, vigorously whisk the egg whites. Add salt, pepper, and garlic powder, until frothy. Whisk in the parmesan cheese. *You can sub out and use shredded cheddar or crumbled feta. For subs increase the amount to ¼ cup. (Your macros will need to be adjusted. Use a food tracking app to recalculate them with the substitutes).
3. Using a spatula, fold the green onions and tomatoes into the egg whites.
4. Lightly spray the skillet with pan spray (i.e. olive oil spray). This is a low-calorie way to cook instead of using butter. If you do not feel like you get enough daily fat from protein choices, you can use one tsp. butter or MCT oil to grease the pan instead of the spray. (Adjust your grams of fat in the macros).
5. Pour the omelette mixture into the pan and slowly increase your heat to medium while cooking. Lift and tilt the skillet to spread the mixture evenly.
6. As soon as the edges start to set, place your spatula under the omelette and lift and tilt the skillet and repeat a few times to evenly spread and cook it.
7. Once your omelette looks cooked and the top isn't runny, you can fold in the sides and flip it.
8. Once you flip your omelette let it cook for 30 seconds more. Then turn off the heat.

Tips: Instead of flipping your omelette you can place a skillet cover over it to allow it to steam cook it and then fold in the sides. When cooking eggs, medium low heat works best so the bottom doesn't burn. Eggs will cook differently depending on whether you use gas or electric heat. Gas tends to cook food more evenly. This is why chefs prefer to use gas burners to cook with. Garnish your omelette with some of the chopped green onion, tomatoes. Enjoy!

BREAKFAST RECIPE 2 ⭐
Egg White Bites

PREP TIME: 10 MINUTES

COOK TIME: 22 MINUTES

READY IN: 32 MINUTES

SERVINGS: 6 Egg Bites

CALORIES 35 PER EGG BITE

MACROS:

CARBS 15g

PROTEIN 58g

FAT 12g

SUGAR 2g

INGREDIENTS

- 1 1/3 CUPS LIQUID EGG WHITES OR 12 EGG WHITES*
- ¼ CUP FINELY DICED RED BELL PEPPER
- ¼ CUP MONTERREY JACK CHEESE
- ¼ CUP COTTAGE CHEESE 2-4%
- ¼ CUP SPINACH, FINELY CHOPPED
- 1 TBS GREEN ONION FINELY CHOPPED
- ½ TSP HOT SAUCE (TOBASCO SAUCE)
- ¼ TSP GARLIC POWDER
- SALT TO TASTE
- FRESHLY GROUND BLACK PEPPER TO TASTE

NOTES: *Egg white bites are a great way to get in a healthy source of protein and carbs while staying low on calories. You can substitute the Monterrey Jack cheese for cheese of choice. Make sure to adjust the macros and calories for the recipe. The spinach and red bell pepper add nice flavor and are a good source of micronutrients. These bites are also great to meal prep for eating healthy on the go.*

MEAL PREP TIP:

- Shop for egg whites and store in fridge for easy prep.
- Cut veggies and shred the cheese a few days before hand and store in the fridge for use when prepping meals.
- Store extra egg bites in a sealed container in the fridge for up to five days.
- For longer storage (two-three months), wrap bites in plastic wrap & place in sealed container, place in the freezer.
- To reheat bites: wrap in damp paper towel, cook in the microwave until warm.

STEPS

1. Preheat the oven to 350 degrees.
2. Add egg whites, hot sauce, garlic powder, salt, and pepper to a large bowl with a spout. Whisk until combined.
3. Mix in the cheeses, bell pepper, spinach, and green onions. Stir until combined.
4. Spray a six well muffin pan (or 12 wells if doubling the recipe) with non-stick cooking spray.
5. Pour egg mix evenly into cups and bake at 350 degrees for 20-22 minutes, or until the eggs set and they are no longer jiggly.
6. Remove from oven, turn off the heat and use a silicon spatula to remove the bites.
7. Garnish with more of the finely chopped green onion if desired.
8. Serve while warm and enjoy!

    *If using whole egg whites, store the yolks in the fridge in a sealed container for other recipes. Egg yolks can be stored for up to two days. Add a little water to the container to prevent them from drying out.

BREAKFAST RECIPE 3 ⭐

Egg White Crepes

PREP TIME: 5 MINUTES

COOK TIME: 5 MINUTES

READY IN: 10 MINUTES

SERVINGS: 2 CREPES

CALORIES 120 EACH CREPE

CALORIES FILLING 89 PER CREPE

INGREDIENTS

- 1 CUP EGG WHITES
- ¼ TSP KOSHER SALT
- ¼ CUP OAT FLOUR
- ¼ CUP UNSWEETENED ALMOND MILK
- 1 TSP VANILLA
- 1 TBS SUGAR FREE MAPLE SYRUP

FILLING

- ½ CUP BLUEBERRIES
- ½ CUP STRAWBERRIES
- ¼ CUP *TRUWHIP*®

Drizzle on my yummy low calorie (90 calories for 2 Tbs) peanut butter syrup. Recipe is under sauces.

MACROS

CREPES	FILLLING
CARBS 22g	CARBS 51g
PROTEIN 31g	PROTEIN 1g
FAT 3g	FAT 2g
SUGAR 2g	SUGAR 9g

NOTES: Crepes are an easy to assemble meal and provide a healthy source of protein. The berry filling is a good way to get in micronutrients. The crepes are also a good option to have as a snack between meals, to satisfy your sweet craving.

STEPS

1. Wash and dry your fruit. Cut the strawberries in half.
2. Mix wet ingredients in a large bowl with spout.
3. Mix in oat flour and salt to taste.
4. Whisk mixture until frothy.
5. Heat an 8-inch skillet with one or two tsp. MCT oil, on the stove for one minute on low heat. *Butter can be used but will be higher in fat and calories.
6. Pour 1/3 the batter mixture into the skillet. Cook for one to two minutes, until set.
7. Flip your crepe with a silicon spatula, cook for 40 seconds until the crepe is cooked through.
8. Remove crepe from skillet, re grease your pan and repeat with remaining batter, 1/3 at a time.
9. Place crepe on plate and fill with some of the berries. You can use some as a garnish.
10. Add ½ the *TruWhip*® to each crepe (about two Tbs each).
11. Fold crepe and drizzle with the peanut butter syrup. Enjoy!

*If fat loss is a goal enter the amount of MCT oil or butter you use into your food tracking app.

Tips: Crepes can take longer to make because they need to cook one at a time. Make sure your skillet is warm and greased, but not too hot that the crepes will burn. You can use the base recipe for crepes and add any type of filling you like, sweet or savory. Once you have made your crepes, they can store in a sealed container for up to four days. Place in damp paper towel and microwave until warm to reheat them.

BREAKFAST RECIPE 4 ⭐

Protein Blueberry Pancakes

PREP TIME: 5 MINUTES

COOK TIME: 10 MINUTES

READY IN: 15 MINUTES

SERVINGS: 2 PANCAKES

CALORIES 125 PER PANCAKE

MACROS FOR TOTAL RECIPE:

CARBS 35g
PROTEIN 42g
FAT 3g
SUGAR 11g

INGREDIENTS

- 4 EGG WHITES
- 1 TBS SUGAR FREE ALMOND MILK
- 1 SCOOP VANILLA PROTEIN POWDER*
- ½ MASHED RIPE BANANA
- ¼ CUP BLUEBERRIES (fresh or frozen)

TOPPINGS:

SUGAR FREE MAPLE SYRUP OR TRUWHIP®

(Toppings are optional and not included in the macros).

NOTES: These tasty pancakes are a healthy source of protein and carbs. The blueberries are a great source of micronutrients. If you do not have ripe banana available, or want less natural sugar in the recipe, you can sub it out with ¼ cup of sugar free apple sauce.

This is a good meal to east post workout because it provides carbs for strength and energy, plus protein for muscle growth.

* I use *Devotion* as my go to protein because it tastes great, contains whey protein isolate and micellar casein, plus digestive enzymes. It's also designed to be used for baking, so it's perfect for using in my recipes. In this recipe I use Angel Food Cake flavor. You can find the link to *Devotion* on my website: Claremorrow.com under *My Favorites*

STEPS

1. Whisk together the egg whites and the protein powder.
2. Stir in mashed banana (or applesauce), and most of the blueberries. Set some aside to garnish the pancakes or the plate with.
3. Add almond milk to thin the mixture, if needed.
4. Heat a non-stick pan or electric griddle on medium low heat, lightly spray with pan spray.
5. Pour half your mixture in a circle, on the pan or griddle, to make one pancake.
6. Cook on medium for two to three minutes until top is bubbly, then flip your pancake over to cook the other side, usually for one to two minutes.
7. Remove the pancake, respray the pan, repeat with remaining batter.
8. This recipe yields two medium pancakes.
9. Turn off the heat and plate the pancakes.
10. Drizzle on sugar free maple syrup. You can also top with a little TruWhip ®instead of the syrup or eat them plain. Enjoy!

BREAKFAST RECIPE 5

 Buttery Biscuit with Egg or Jam

PREP TIME: 5 MINUTES

COOK TIME: 25 MINUTES

READY IN: 30 MINUTES

SERVINGS: 1 BISCUIT WITH EGG

MACROS

BISCUIT	EGGS
CARBS 6g	CARBS 2g
PROTEIN 26g	PROTEIN 17g
FAT 2g	FAT 5g
SUGAR 1g	SUGAR 1g

CALORIES 130 PER BISCUIT/129 FOR THE EGGS

INGREDIENTS

- 30g (one scoop) *DEVOTION PROTEIN* BUTTERY BLEND FLAVOR*
- 30g ZERO FAT PLAIN GREEK YOGURT
- 3 EGG WHITES
- 1 WHOLE EGG
- ¼ TSP SEA SALT
- ¼ TSP FRESHLY GROUND BLACK PEPPER
- 1 TSP CHOPPED CHIVES (OPTIONAL).

NOTES: *These biscuits come out light and fluffy and taste so good! The buttery blend protein gives it a "melt in your mouth flavor" while allowing you to get in more protein for the day. You can make these biscuits with egg or spread on your favorite sugar free jelly or jam. I use Good Good® brand. You can find the link for them on my Amazon page or use your personal favorite.* **If using jam instead of egg, make sure to adjust your macros.**

*I use *Devotion* as my go-to source for quality protein. It contains digestive enzymes which can help with bloating and constipation. The *Buttery Blend* flavor is hard to find in other protein powders. You can find the link to *Devotion* on my website: Claremorrow.com under "My Favorites."

You can use your preferred protein or your favorite vegan protein if you follow a vegan diet. Look for one that is good for baking.

STEPS

1. Preheat the oven to 350 degrees.
2. In medium size bowl, add in the scoop of protein, a pinch of sea salt, and the Greek yogurt.
3. Mix with a wooden spoon or your hands. Dust your spoon or hands in almond flower to help prevent the dough from sticking while mixing. DO NOT OVERWORK THE DOUGH.
4. Let the dough rest while you prepare your eggs.
5. In a bowl lightly whisk three egg whites and one whole egg. Salt and pepper to taste.
6. Take a ceramic cooking dish and spray with nonstick pan spray, place the biscuit inside, and place in the center rack of the oven. Set the timer for 25 minutes.
7. While the biscuit is cooking, heat a pan on your stove on medium, spray with nonstick cooking spray. Add in chopped chives (optional) let them cook for 10 seconds.
8. Add in your egg mix. Scramble eggs gently with silicon spatula. Cook until done.
9. Check your biscuit after 20 minutes in the oven. Cook time can vary depending on if you have gas or electric heat. The middle should slice clean with a knife.
10. Remove the biscuit from the oven. Turn off heat. Slice your biscuit, place the egg inside or spread on your favorite jam. Enjoy!

BREAKFAST RECIPE 6 ⭐⭐

Steel Cut Oats

PREP TIME: 5 MINUTES

COOK TIME: 25 MINUTES

READY IN: 30 MINUTES

SERVINGS: 1

CALORIES 150 PLAIN OATS
WITH BLUEBERRIES 170
WITH PROTEIN POWDER 230

INGREDIENTS

- STEEL CUT OATS
- MONK FRUIT SUGAR
- KOSHER SALT
- ¼ CUP BLUBERRIES (Use frozen or fresh).
- ½ SCOOP CINNAMON FLAVOR PROTEIN POWDER*
- USE REAL CINNAMON IF YOU SKIP THE PROTEIN POWDER

MACROS: OATS	BLUEBERRIES
CARBS 29g	CARBS 5g
PROTEIN 5g	PROTEIN .3g
FAT 3g	FAT .12g
SUGAR 0g	SUGAR 4g

NOTES: Oats are a staple of my diet. I pretty much have them every morning. They're a healthy source of carbs, low fat, and it's easy to top them with blueberries or strawberries to get in micronutrients. You can also add in some protein powder to get in extra protein for the day. *I use Devotion Sinful Cinnamon flavor. **You can use a vegan protein option if you are on a vegan diet.**

MACROS: ½ SCP PROTEIN POWDER

CARBS 1g
PROTEIN 10g
FAT 1g
SUGAR 0g
CALORIES 60

COOKING TIPS:

- I use steel cut oats rather than quick or instant oats to make this recipe. Steel cut oats are slower digesting which is easier on our body. Plus there are studies that show instant oats can cause a bigger spike in our insulin levels. Steel cut oats do take longer to prepare but the benefits are worth it.
- I cook my oats in larger batches and store them in the refrigerator to have for the next day. You can also freeze them in a sealed container for longer storage.

STEPS

1. Place saucepan on the stove and add two cups of water. You can use less water for thicker oats.
2. Add ½ cup oats and a pinch or two of kosher salt. Mix lightly with a spoon.
3. Turn the heat to medium low and bring your mixture up to a simmer.
4. Cover the saucepan and let your oats simmer for five minutes. Add one tsp. Monk Fruit Sugar and sprinkle in one tsp of cinnamon. To taste.
5. If you are using the *Sinful Cinnamon* protein powder, skip the regular cinnamon. Or you can use plain or vanilla flavored protein powder and use the regular cinnamon.
6. Cover your saucepan again and let your oats simmer for 15 more minutes, stirring occasionally.
7. Remove from heat when you like the consistency. Remember they will thicken more as they cool. Turn off the heat.
8. Add oats to your bowl and add some blueberries or strawberries to the top and stir those in. Enjoy!

BREAKFAST RECIPE 7 ⭐

The Barbell Breakfast

PREP TIME: 10 MINUTES

COOK TIME: 10 MINUTES

READY IN: 20 MINUTES

INGREDIENTS

- ½ CUP COOKED OATS (USE THE STEEL CUT OATS RECIPE. OMIT PROTEIN POWDER).
- 1 BISCUIT (USE THE BUTTERY BISCUIT RECIPE WHICH INCLUDES PROTEIN POWDER).

FOR THE EGGS

- 3 EGG WHITES
- 1 WHOLE EGG

OPTIONAL TOPPINGS:

- ¼ CUP BLUEBERRIES (FROZEN OR FRESH)
- SUGAR FREE JAM

To give more flavor to your eggs, you can add a dash of my low-calorie salsa, or hot sauce. Recipes can be found on the sauces page.

THE MACROS IN THIS RECIPE DO NOT INCLUDE THE PROTEIN POWDER IN THE OATS, SINCE IT'S NOT NEEDED, DUE TO PROTEIN IN THE EGGS & BISCUIT

SERVINGS: ½ cup oats, 1 buttery biscuit, 1 whole egg, 3 egg whites.

CALORIES 150 OATS, 130 BISCUIT, 129 EGGS

TOTAL CALORIES: 409

WITH ¼ BLUEBBERRIES, ADD 20 CALORIES TO TOTAL.

MACROS:
CARBS 36g
PROTEIN 49g
FAT 10g
SUGAR 5g

ADD FOR BLUEBERRIES
CARBS 5g
PROTEIN 3g
FAT 1g
SUGAR 4g.

NOTES: *This is one of my favorite breakfast combos that I like to have as a pre workout meal. Remember you can adjust the portion size and macros for your stats. This meal provides protein, plenty of carbs, micronutrients, and is very satiating!*

STEPS

1. For the egg whites you can make a scramble simply by whisking them, adding salt and pepper to taste. Cook in a heated skillet sprayed with pan spray over medium heat.
2. For the whole egg you can prepare it any way you like. Hard or soft boiled, sunny side up, or over easy. Just make sure to cook the egg using pan spray rather than melting an unmeasured amount of butter or margarine since the calories from oils add up fast.
3. If you need to get more fat in your diet (if fat loss is not a goal) then you can use a small amount of butter to cook with. Just make sure to enter it in your food tracking app.
4. To assemble your breakfast plate your eggs, along with a buttery biscuit and a bowl of oats. You can top the oats with blueberries or strawberries.
5. Sugar free strawberry jam can be used on your biscuit. I use *Good Good*® brand.
6. Both the steel cut oats and the buttery biscuit are items that can be used in meal prep. They can be made in larger batches and stored in the fridge for several days. Reheat them before serving. This makes the prep time for *The Barbell Breakfast* easy to do in the morning since you will just cook the eggs and assemble. Enjoy!

LUNCH RECIPE 1

 ## *Cloud Bread Club Sandwich*

PREP TIME: 10 MINUTES

COOK TIME: 30 MINUTES

READY IN: 40 MINUTES

SERVINGS: 1 SANDWICH

MACROS

2 SLICES OF BREAD	WHOLE SANDWICH
CARBS 2g	CARBS 6g
PROTEIN 6g	PROTEIN 40g
FAT 2g	FAT 7g
SUGAR 1g	SUGAR 2g
CALORIES: 63	**CALORIES:** 375

INGREDIENTS

CLOUD BREAD
- 3 LARGE EGG WHITES & 1 YOLK
- 2 TBS 0% GREEK YOGURT
- ¼ TSP CREAM OF TARTAR
- 1/8 TSP SEA SALT

LAYERS SHOWN
- ROMAINE LETTUCE
- TOMATO
- CUCUMBER
- BACON BITS (Optional)
- 6 OZ. SHREDDED COOKED CHICKEN

CONDIMENTS
- YELLOW MUSTARD
- VEGAN MAYO (less fat & lo cal).

NOTES: Cloud Bread has less calories and carbs than most commercial made bread, and it's high in protein. You can easily meal prep with Cloud Bread. Cook up a bunch and store it in a sealed container in your fridge for several days. You can freeze it for longer storage.

A traditional Club Sandwich is made with bacon. To get that same flavor without all the fat that use some bacon bits instead.

You can customize your sandwich with layers you like. Some options are pickles, avocado (has higher fat and more calories but is a healthier source of fat if you need to get more in your diet), sprouts, and sliced turkey.

Make sure to adjust your macros for any changes.

CLOUD BREAD STEPS

This recipe yields six slices of bread.

1. Preheat the oven to 300 degrees.
2. Separate the egg whites from the yolks.
3. Put the egg whites in a big bowl and add in the cream of tartar. Use an electric hand blender on high speed to whip them until stiff peaks form. (Four-9 Minutes).
4. In a medium bowl combine **one yolk,** the Greek Yogurt, and the salt.
5. Gently fold the yogurt-yolk mixture, into the egg whites until even color. **Do not over blend.**
6. Line a dark baking sheet with parchment paper and pour the mixture into six even circles (around 4" diameter). Use the back of a spoon to spread out the batter.
7. Bake on the middle rack for 30 minutes, until golden brown throughout.
8. Remove the bread from the oven and turn off the heat. Assemble your sandwich. Enjoy!

LUNCH RECIPE 2 ⭐

Baked Chicken Wings

PREP TIME: 10 MINUTES

COOK TIME: 40 MINUTES

READY IN: 50 MINUTES

INGREDIENTS

SERVINGS: 8 Medium Wings

MACROS

CHICKEN	RANCH DIP
CARBS 2g	CARBS 4g
PROTEIN 35g	PROTEIN 12g
FAT 7g	FAT 0g
SUGAR 0g	SUGAR 4g
CALORIES: 370	**CALORIES:** 70

CHICKEN
- FRESH WINGS (A PARTY TRAY IS BEST BECAUSE THEY ARE ALREADY CUT INTO FLATS & DRUMS).
- SPRAY OIL (Avocado or coconut oil).

SEASONING
- KOSHER SALT
- FRESH GROUND BLACK PEPPER
- GARLIC POWDER or ONION POWDER
- PAPRIKA (Original or smoked).

RANCH DIP
- ½ CUP GREEK YOGURT 0%
- 2 TBS RANCH SEASONING
- FRESH DILL (Optional).

NOTES: *For extra crispy wings, bake them for 30 minutes at 400 turn down the heat to 170 degrees and let them bake for 30-45 minutes more. Serve with fresh celery.*

These are easy to make in batches for meal prep.

Instead of ranch dressing, I like to make my own healthier version using 0% Greek Yogurt mixed with ranch seasoning. I prefer *Fage* brand; You can use your favorite.

You can also use a BBQ or Honey Mustard sauce to dip the wings in. I have some sugar free ones on my *Amazon* Page under Food Swaps. I really like the *G. Hughes* brand or use your favorite sugar free sauce.

STEPS

1. Preheat the oven to 400 degrees.
2. Wash the chicken wings and set them aside.
3. Mix your spices of choice in a bowl.
4. Take a baking sheet and fit it with a wire rack.
5. Generously spray your wings with the oil. Salt and pepper to taste.
6. Place the wings on the wire rack and sprinkle on your seasonings. Turn them and season the other side.
7. Place the wings in the center rack and bake for 35-40 minutes.
8. For the ranch dip, mix ½ cup Greek Yogurt with some of the ranch seasoning. Add a pinch of the dill and mix. Place in the fridge for 15 minutes for the flavor to set up.
9. Check your wings after 35 minutes. They should be golden brown.
10. Take wings out of the oven and turn off the heat. Enjoy!

LUNCH RECIPE 3

Protein Mac & Cheese

PREP TIME: 10 MINUTES

COOK TIME: 15 MINUTES

READY IN: 25 MINUTES

SERVINGS: 10 OUNCES

MACROS
CARBS 54g
PROTEIN 50g
FAT 6g
SUGAR 4g

CALORIES: 395

INGREDIENTS

- 1 ½ CUPS ELBOW PASTA
- 3 OZ OF *PHILADELPIHIAS LIGHTEST*
- ¼ CUP ALMOND MILK (Unsweetened).
- 3 TBS PASTA WATER
- 1/8 CUP REDUCED FAT CHEDDAR CHEESE (Block style). *
- ¼ CUP OF CORNFLAKES
- 1 SCP *DEVOTION* PROTEIN BUTTERY BLEND FLAVOR**

SEASONINGS

- KOSHER SALT
- FRESH GROUND BLACK PEPPER
- ANY OTHERS YOU LIKE

NOTES: *This healthier version of mac n cheese is so good! The Philadelphia Lightest gives it the creamy texture with less calories. Pair this dish with a side salad. *I use block cheese and shred it myself because it melts much better than the shredded variety due to the anti-caking preservatives.*

**Adding the protein is optional but it is a great way to sneak in some extra protein for the day. I use *Devotion* as my go to protein because it tastes great, contains whey protein isolate and micellar casein, plus digestive enzymes. It's also designed to be used for baking, so it's perfect for using in my recipes. You can find the link to *Devotion* on my website: Claremorrow.com under *My Favorites*. If you follow a vegan diet, you can use vegan protein and vegan cheeses in this recipe. Make sure the protein is suitable for baking with.

STEPS

1. Preheat the oven to 325 degrees.
2. Bring a large pot filled with water and a dash of kosher salt to a boil. Cook your pasta per instructions **remove from heat one minute early** so it is *al dente*.
3. Scoop out 1/4 cup of the pasta water before draining it. Set aside.
4. Make the sauce by adding the *Philadelphia Lightest* and the almond milk to a pot. Boil over medium heat on the stove for about five minutes. Stir while cooking.
5. Take a baking dish and spray the inside lightly with cooking oil, add the pasta, three Tbs. pasta water, and the protein powder. Mix to combine.
6. Pour the cheese sauce over your pasta. Add salt and pepper to taste and stir.
7. Top the dish with the shredded cheddar.
8. Crush up the corn flakes and add to the top.
9. Bake 15-20 minutes. Turn off the heat and let the dish cool. Enjoy!

LUNCH RECIPE 4
Tasty Tuna Wrap

PREP TIME: 15 MINUTES

COOK TIME: 10 MINUTES

READY IN: 25 MINUTES

SERVINGS: 2 WRAPS

CALORIES: 229

MACROS TOTAL RECIPE

- CARBS 12g
- PROTEIN 51g
- FAT 2g
- SUGAR 8g

INGREDIENTS

CLOUD BREAD WRAP
- 5 EGG WHITES
- 1 TBS CORNSTARCH

TUNA
- 5 OZ TUNA PACKED **IN WATER.**
- 2 TBS 0 % GREEK YOGURT
- ¼ GREEN APPLE
- ROMAINE LETTUCE (Optional).
- CHOPPED NUTS *(Optional. Not included in the macros).

NOTES: *You can use tuna in the pouch or tuna in the can for this recipe. Just make sure it is packed in water not oil, for less fat and calories.*

Replacing mayo in your tuna with Greek Yogurt, is a healthy, yet tasty way to lower the calories. It also cuts out a bunch of preservatives found in mayo.

This recipe uses Romaine lettuce as a layer between the wrap and the tuna which helps prevent the bread from getting soggy. The lettuce is optional. or you can use your preferred kind instead.

Chopped walnuts or another type of nut, can be added for more flavor, or if you need to get more natural fats in your diet. Adjust your macros when adding them in.

STEPS

1. Preheat the oven to 350 degrees.
2. Take out a baking pan and line with parchment paper.
3. Place egg whites in a large mixing bowl and add in the corn starch. Use a hand mixer and beat the egg whites on high speed from four minutes to nine minutes until stiff peaks form. It can take a while so be patient.
4. Pour the mixture onto the pan and spread it out with a spatula.
5. Bake for 8-10 minutes. Or until light golden brown. Turn off heat and set the bread to the side to cool. Or store in fridge for later use.
6. Open tuna and drain the water. Add to mixing bowl with two Tbs yogurt.
7. Wash your apple (peel if you want). Dice ¼ of the apple and add to the tuna.
8. Wash a few Romaine lettuce leaves and pat dry. Take your cloud bread wrap and line the inside with the lettuce.
9. Spread on your tuna salad. Add nuts if desired. Roll it up and cut in half. Enjoy!

LUNCH RECIPE 5

Cloud Bread Turkey Burger

PREP TIME: 10 MINUTES

COOK TIME: 30 MINUTES

READY IN: 40 MINUTES

SERVINGS: 1 BURGER

MACROS

BURGER	BUN
CARBS 1g	CARBS 2g
PROTEIN 18g	PROTEIN 6g
FAT 2g	FAT 2g
SUGAR 1g	SUGAR 1g
CALORIES: 92	**CALORIES: 63**

INGREDIENTS

CLOUD BREAD
- 3 LARGE EGG WHITES & 1 YOLK
- 2 TBS 0% GREEK YOGURT
- ¼ TSP CREAM OF TARTAR
- 1/8 TSP SEA SALT

MAKES 6 BURGERS
- 1 LB. LEAN GROUND TURKEY
- 1 CUP FINELY SHREDDED MEDIUM SIZE ZUCCHINI
- 1 LARGE GARLIC CLOVE, GRATED
- 1 TSP CUMIN
- ½ TSP KOSHER SALT
- ¼ TSP GROUND BLACK PEPPER

Notes: Lean ground turkey is one of my favorite sources of protein. You can use it for a variety of recipes, from burgers to rice bowls to lettuce

For condiments with less calories, stick with yellow mustard, or 0% Greek yogurt with ranch seasoning. Or try salsa. Avoid ketchup since it has more sugar.

Add your favorite toppings to the burger. Lettuce, tomato, pickles, or hummus are healthy options. Make sure to adjust your macros for the toppings.

Steps

1. **FOR THE BREAD** Preheat the oven to 300 degrees.
2. Separate the egg whites from the yolks.
3. Put the egg whites in a big bowl and add in the cream of tartar. Use an electric hand blender on high speed to whip them until stiff peaks form. (four to 9 Minutes).
4. In a medium bowl, combine **one yolk,** the Greek Yogurt, and the salt.
5. Gently fold the yogurt-yolk mixture into the egg whites until even color.
6. Line a dark baking sheet with parchment paper and pour the mixture into six even circles. Use the back of a spoon to make even circles about 4" in diameter.
7. Bake on the middle rack for 30 minutes, until golden brown throughout.
8. Remove from oven turn off the heat and allow them to cool before using.
9. **FOR THE BURGERS** Place the ground turkey, zucchini, garlic, salt, pepper, and cumin in a bowl. Mix thoroughly by hand.
10. Portion the mixture out into six sections. Roll each section into a ball and press flat into a patty shape. Indent the middle slightly with a spoon, so edges are slightly higher.
11. Pre heat a skillet on medium heat. Add 1 ½ Tsp. MCT oil. Add three patties, cook on low heat for about five minutes per side. Repeat with the next three patties. Once cooked assemble your burger.
12. These burgers can be cooked on a grill. Place them in the freezer for 10 minutes before grilling to help them hold their shape. Enjoy!

LUNCH RECIPE 6
Cloud Bread Pizza

PREP TIME: 10 MINUTES

COOK TIME: 35 MINUTES

READY IN: 45 MINUTES

SERVINGS: 1 MEDIUM PIZZA

CALORIES: 220

MACROS: PIZZA AS SHOWN
- CARBS 14g
- PROTEIN 42g
- FAT 12g
- SUGAR 3g

INGREDIENTS

CLOUD BREAD CRUST
- 3 LARGE EGG WHITES & 1 YOLK
- 2 TBS 0% GREEK YOGURT
- ¼ TSP CREAM OF TARTAR
- 1/8 TSP SEA SALT
- GARLIC POWDER
- OREGANO
- GROUND BLACK PEPPER

RED SAUCE
- NO SALT ADDED TOMATO SAUCE
- 1 TSP MINCED GARLIC
- ¼ OF A YELLOW ONION
- 2 BAY LEAVES

TOPPPINGS
- 6 OZ CHEESE (Pizza blend). **
- VEGGIES OF CHOICE

NOTES: *Cloud bread is great to make in batches and can store in the fridge for up to one week! This helps cut back on the prep time for meals and can help you stay on track with your diet goals.*

*MCT oil or olive oil used to sauté the onions adds 110 calories and 14 grams of fat to this recipe! If fat loss is a goal use cooking spray and a little water instead.

To make the red sauce: Peel and slice the ¼ onion. Place a saucepan on the stove on medium heat. Spray with pan spray add in a little water. Sauté the onion until it's caramelized. Add in an 8 oz can of the tomato sauce, add in the minced garlic, add the bay leaf, stir, and simmer over low heat for 8-10 minutes.

STEPS

FOR THE CLOUD BREAD CRUST

1. Preheat the oven to 300 degrees.
2. Separate the egg whites from the yolks.
3. Put the egg whites in a big bowl and add in the cream of tartar. Use an electric hand blender on high speed to whip them until stiff peaks form (4-9 minutes).
4. In a medium bowl, combine **one yolk,** the Greek Yogurt, and the salt.
5. Gently fold the yogurt-yolk mixture, into the egg whites until even color.
6. Add in your spices for the crust (oregano, garlic powder, black pepper).
7. Line a dark baking sheet with parchment paper and pour the mixture into a circle in the middle. Use the back of a spoon to spread out the dough to the size you like.
8. Bake on the middle rack for 30 minutes, until golden brown, throughout.
9. Remove from oven. Take a wire baking rack and place the cloud bread on top.
10. Spread a layer of red sauce on your cloud bread crust.
11. Add your cheese and any other toppings. **Adjust macros for additional toppings.**
12. Put the rack in the oven (or place the pizza in the air fryer) for a few more minutes until the cheese is melted. Enjoy! **Use less cheese to cut back on the fat and calories

LUNCH RECIPE 7

 Protein Pasta With Red Sauce

PREP TIME: 10 MINUTES

COOK TIME: 15 MINUTES

READY IN: 25 MINUTES

SERVINGS: 8 OZ SERVING OF PASTA

MACROS:
CARBS 35g
PROTEIN 50g
FAT 3g
SUGAR 3g

CALORIES: 320

INGREDIENTS

PASTA
- 8 OUNCES OF PENNE PASTA
- ½ TSP KOSHER SALT

RED SAUCE
- NO SALT ADDED TOMATO SAUCE
- 1 TSP MINCED GARLIC
- ¼ YELLOW ONION SLICED THIN
- 2 BAY LEAVES

PROTEIN
- 1 SCOOP *DEVOTION* PROTEIN BUTTERY BLEND FLAVOR

NOTES: This pasta dish is perfect for a mid-day meal. It's packed with protein and carbs and is a lighter meal so that you don't end up with that food coma feeling late in the day.

To Make the Red Sauce: Peel and slice the onion. Place a saucepan on the stove on medium heat. **Spray with pan spray. Add 2 TBS water.** Sauté the onion until it's caramelized. Add in an 8 oz can of the tomato sauce, the minced garlic, the bay leaf and stir. Simmer over low heat for 8-10 minutes.

*If you use MCT or Olive Oil to sauté onions, that adds 110 calories and 14 grams of fat to this recipe. If fat loss is a goal, use pan spray instead.

* I use *Devotion* as my go to protein because it tastes great, contains whey protein isolate and micellar casein, plus digestive enzymes. It's also designed to be used for baking, so it's perfect for using in my recipes. You can find the link to *Devotion* on my website: Claremorrow.com under *My Favorites*. If you follow a vegan diet, you can use a vegan protein in this recipe. Make sure it is suitable for baking.

STEPS

1. Take a large pot and fill with water. Use four times the amount of water than pasta to prevent it from getting starchy while cooking.
2. Add the kosher salt and a few sprays of cooking spray to the water. Bring to a low boil.
3. Add in your pasta. Follow the directions on the package. Make sure to stir your pasta while it's cooking to prevent it from sticking together.
4. While the pasta is cooking, make your red sauce. (See steps above).
5. Once your pasta is done, set aside ¼ cup pasta water to mix with your protein powder. If you forget you can use regular water. Pasta water makes it creamier.
6. Drain your pasta and add to a bowl.
7. Pour a scoop of the protein powder in a bowl and slowly mix in the ¼ cup pasta water.
8. Add in your red sauce and stir until blended.
9. Pour the red sauce over the pasta. You can add some grated parmesan cheese to top it off. Just remember to add that to your macros. Enjoy!

LUNCH RECIPE 8
Air Fried Flounder

Plain   *Breaded*

PREP TIME: 10 MINUTES

COOK TIME: 15 MINUTES

READY IN: 25 MINUTES

SERVINGS: 2 FILETS

MACROS:

PLAIN	BREADED
CARBS 2g	CARBS 35g
PROTEIN 23g	PROTEIN 37g
FAT 2g	FAT 6g
SUGAR 1g	SUGAR 4g
CALORIES: 145	**CALORIES:** 325

INGREDIENTS

FISH
- 2 FLOUNDER FILETS FROZEN OR FRESH. (1 LB.)
- 1 SMALL LEMON
- KOSHER SALT
- GROUND BLACK PEPPER
- PARSLEY FLAKES (To garnish).

BREADING (optional)
- 2 EGG WHITES
- ½ CUP *PANKO* BREADCRUMBS

NOTES: *Seafood is a great way to get protein in your diet from a healthy source. White fish like flounder and cod are the best choices because they are lower in fat and calories than other fattier types of fish, like salmon. I'm not saying to never have them just be careful of how often when fat loss is a goal.*

A great way to give your fish flavor without adding a lot of calories is to use sugar free sauce. I like the *G. Hughes* brand. The Sweet Chili sauce goes great with this recipe. You can find the sauces on my *Amazon* page. You can also make homemade tartar sauce* with 0% Greek Yogurt mixed with 1 Tsp. relish.

STEPS

1. Place a cooking liner in the air fryer.
2. Take the flounder filets gently rinse them and pat them dry.
3. Spray the pan liner with a little cooking spray. Place the filets on the liner. Salt and pepper to taste. (I cook my fish unseasoned and use sauces for flavoring).
4. Place the pan liner with the fish in the air fryer. Cook at 400 degrees for 12-15 minutes. Flip the fish once during cooking. Season the other side.
5. Cook the fish until it's flaky and develops a golden-brown crust.

BREADED FISH VERSION (MAKES A GREAT KIDS MEAL TOO).

1. Add two egg whites into a bowl. Salt and pepper to taste. Mix well.
2. Add the *Panko* breadcrumbs to a bowl.
3. Dip the fish into the egg whites and then into the breadcrumbs. Coat both sides.
4. Follow steps 4 and 5 from above. Serve either recipe with lemon slices. Garnish with parsley flakes. Enjoy!

DINNER RECIPE 1

 Ground Turkey Shepard's Pie

PREP TIME: 20 MINUTES

COOK TIME: 20 MINUTES

READY IN: 40 MINUTES

SERVINGS: 8

CALORIES PER SERVING: 290

MACROS PER SERVING:

CARBS 29g
PROTEIN 30g
FAT 2g
SUGAR 1g

INGREDIENTS

- 2 LBS. OF 99% LEAN TURKEY
- 4-5 MEDIUM SIZE POTATOES OF CHOICE. (You can use yellow, red, or russet potatoes).
- 1 MEDIUM YELLOW ONION
- 1 CAN OF TOMATO PASTE 9 OZ.
- ¼ CUP WORCESTERSHIRE SAUCE
- 1 CUP BEEF BROTH
- 1 BAG OF FROZEN MIXED VEGGIES OF CHOICE. (approx. 16 ounces).
- SALT & PEPPER TO TASTE

NOTES: *This low-calorie recipe is one of my favorites. It not only tastes delicious but it's high in protein and carbs and is satiating, so it fills you up.*

The trick to keeping this recipe low calorie is to use a leaner type of ground meat for your protein source. Ground turkey is a great choice because it is leaner than beef, yet it is flavorful and goes well with the potatoes and veggies.

For a vegan version of this recipe use a mixture of chopped mushrooms and lentils for the protein. Use vegetable broth instead of beef. Make sure to adjust the macros if you are doing a vegan option.

STEPS

1. Rinse the potatoes and chop into small pieces. Peeling is optional. Take a large saucepan, add your potatoes, some salt, and bring to a boil for about 15-20 minutes, until the potatoes are soft and a little mushy. Drain and set aside.
2. Chop the onion spray some cooking spray into a pan and add the onion.
3. Cook the onions until golden and add in your 2 lbs. of turkey.
4. Mix well and continue to cook over medium heat for 8-10 minutes.
5. Add in the tomato paste, Worcestershire sauce, and beef broth. Mix well.
6. Add in the bag of veggies (after they have slightly thawed if using frozen). Mix everything again. Add in a little water. Salt and pepper to taste.
7. Place the potatoes in a bowl and use a hand blender to mash them up.
8. Take the turkey & veggie mix and add it to a glass (Pyrex) baking dish and spread it out well.
9. Spread a layer of the mashed potatoes on top.
10. Set the oven to broil. Broil at 550 degrees for 10-15 minutes until potatoes start to brown. Enjoy!

DINNER RECIPE 2

False Alarm Chili

PREP TIME: 15 MINUTES

COOK TIME: 30 MINUTES

READY IN: 45 MINUTES

SERVINGS: 4

MACROS PER SERVING:

MEAT & VEGGIES	**WITH BEANS**
CARBS 12g	CARBS 28g
PROTEIN 42g	PROTEIN 48g
FAT 8g	FAT 9g
SUGAR 1g	SUGAR 2g
CALORIES: 320	**CALORIES:** 390

INGREDIENTS

CHILI WITH BISON OR BEEF
- 2 LBS GROUND BISON* OR BEEF
- 2 8 OZ CANS OF TOMATO SAUCE
- 1 SMALL YELLOW ONION
- 1 CUP WATER
- 1 TSP KOSHER SALT
- 1 BOX OF FALSE ALARM MILD CHILI SEASONING**

EXTRAS
- 1 15 OZ CAN OF KIDNEY OR PINTO BEANS (optional).
- 1 15 OZ CAN DICED TOMATOS (DO NOT NEED TO DRAIN).
- 1 MEDIUM GREEN PEPPER

*****NOTES:*** *When a recipe calls for beef as the protein, I usually sub out and use bison because it is leaner and higher in iron than beef. I get my bison directly from a local butcher shop. You can look at your regular grocery store to see if they carry it as well. You can also use venison in this recipe, which is also a leaner than beef, but does not have as much iron as bison.*

****This recipe is for the milder chili using the False Alarm Chili Kit. If you like spicier chili, there is a two Alarm Chili Kit you can use, or follow this recipe and add in a few jalapenos or red pepper to give it more heat.**

To keep this recipe healthier, I do not top the chili with cheese or sour cream. Those toppings really increase the calories. When fat loss is a goal, try to avoid the decadent extras!

STEPS

1. Add the bison or beef to a pan sprayed with cooking spray. Cook on medium heat until brown. Add the salt while it's cooking if desired.
2. Add in the chopped onion and green pepper (if using them in the recipe).
3. Once the meat is brown, remove from heat and drain any fat. Place the meat in a bowl, add one cup of warm water.
4. Add in the two cans of tomato sauce and the seasoning packets from the kit. i.e. oregano, cumin, paprika, dried onion, garlic, and chili powder. Mix it all together. (If you use real onion, you can omit the onion seasoning pack and sprinkle just the garlic powder on your mixture).
5. Add the beans and diced tomato (if using these) and mix well.
6. The kit has a Masa packet for thicker chili. (Optional).
7. Pour your chili mix in a large pot and let simmer on the stove for 30 minutes.
8. Serve while warm and enjoy!

DINNER RECIPE 3 ⭐

Fat Loss Fajitas

PREP TIME: 15 MINUTES

COOK TIME: 20 MINUTES

READY IN: 35 MINUTES

SERVINGS: 2 FAJITAS

MACROS PER FAJITA:

BEEF	CHICKEN
CARBS 20g	CARBS 20g
PROTEIN 28g	PROTEIN 26g
FAT 14g	FAT 8g
SUGAR 1g	SUGAR 1g
CALORIES: 360	**CALORIES: 290**

INGREDIENTS

USE 4 OZ OF MEAT PER FAJITA

- 1 CHICKEN BREAST*
- 1 SMALL FLANK STEAK
- ½ YELLOW ONION
- 1 GREEN BELL PEPPER (small)
- 1 RED BELL PEPPER (small)
- 2 TBS WORCESTERSHIRE SAUCE
- 1 15 OZ CAN OF PINTO BEANS (Low sodium brand).
- LOW CARB TORTILLAS (I prefer *Mr. Tortilla* brand).
- ½ AVOCADO
- SALT & PEPPER TO TASTE

NOTES: **Chicken is a great source of protein. When fat loss is a goal white meat for your recipes is a better choice. Using chicken breast as compared to dark meat, like thighs, means less fat and calories.*

You can do a vegan version of this recipe using tofu instead of meat as your protein source.

Pinto beans are optional. They are a healthy source of carbs. Macros for ½ cup pinto beans are: 99 calories, 6g protein, 17g carbs, 1g fat, 1g sugar.

STEPS

1. Wash the green and red bell peppers. (Yellow bell pepper is fine too). Peel the onion and cut all the veggies into slices.
2. Heat a pan on the stove on medium and spray with cooking spray. Add in the onion and peppers. Add a little water and the Worcestershire sauce. Cook the veggies until they are tender.
3. Heat up your grill. Wash the chicken. Salt and pepper to taste. Cook the steak until it's done to your liking. Make sure the chicken is cooked all the way through. There should be no pink in the center of it.
4. Once the meat is done set it to the side to cool. Slice up the meat.
5. Rince and drain the kidney beans. Measure 4 oz. for this recipe. Save the rest in a jar in the fridge. Place them in a pan and heat them up. Use a potato masher to mash them up. Add a pinch of salt (optional).
6. Cut the avocado in half and scoop out the seed. Score the avocado in its skin and scoop it out with a spoon. Use only one half the avocado for this recipe.
7. Heat the tortilla (place in foil on the grill or cook directly on greases grill).
8. Place the fajita meat and veggies in the tortilla. Top with avocado. Serve with the ½ cup portion of mashed beans on the side. Enjoy!

DINNER RECIPE 4

Healthy Shrimp Scampi

PREP TIME: 10 MINUTES

COOK TIME: 10 MINUTES

READY IN: 20 MINUTES

SERVINGS: 4

MACROS PER SERVING:

CARBS 8g

PROTEIN 25g

FAT 6g

SUGAR 3g

CALORIES: 183

INGREDIENTS

- 1 TBS MCT OIL
- 1 LB LARGE SHRIMP, PEELED AND DE VEINED.
- 1 TSP SEA SALT
- ½ TSP GROUND BLACK PEPPER
- ¼ TSP CRUSHED RE PEPPER FLAKES
- 4 CLOVES MINCED GARLIC
- ¼ CUP LOW SODIUM VEGETABLE BROTH (OR CHICKEN).
- ½ LEMON ZESTED
- ¼ CUP FRESHLY SQUEEZED LEMON JUICE
- 1 LB. ZUCCHINI NOODLES. (SPIRALIZED). USE 2 LARGE ZUCCHINIS.
- ¼ CUP ITALIAN PARSLEY CHOPPED
- 2 TBS FRESHLY GRATE PARMESAN CHEESE

NOTES: Shrimp is an often-overlooked way to get in more protein without a lot of fat and calories. In addition shrimp dishes are easy to make and you can use fresh or frozen shrimp for most recipes. To save time & money buy frozen shrimp in large quantities.

Most scampi dishes have wine as a main ingredient. Some of the alcohol content burns off during cooking but it does increase the calories in the recipe. Because of that I use low sodium vegetable broth as the liquid. This adds flavor without the extra calories. Also your body does not have to pause the breakdown of fats to rid itself of the alcohol, which it sees as a toxin.

This dish is great to serve to family or friends. It can also be used to meal prep for the week. Store unused portions in the fridge in a sealed container.

STEPS

1. Heat the MCT oil in a **large skillet** on medium-low heat.
2. Add in the shrimp, sea salt, pepper, and crushed red pepper flakes. Sauté for four to six minutes, until the shrimp begin to brown and are no longer translucent.
3. Add the garlic to the pan and cook for one minute, stirring frequently.
4. Add in the broth, lemon zest, lemon juice, and zucchini noodles.
5. Bring to a boil and cook for one minute until the shrimp are completely opaque and cooked through and the noodles are softened. Make sure they are coated with the garlic-lemon sauce and warmed through.
6. Remove the skillet from the heat and plate your dishes.
7. Sprinkle each dish with a little of the chopped parsley and a slice of lemon on the side. Top with one tsp parmesan cheese or serve it on the side in a bowl. Enjoy!

DINNER RECIPE 5

 Spaghetti Squash with Turkey

PREP TIME: 10 MINUTES

COOK TIME: 40 MINUTES

READY IN: 50 MINUTES

SERVINGS: 6
MACROS:
6 OZ SERVING SQUASH
8 OZ SERVING SAUCE & TURKEY
CARBS 18g
PROTEIN 48g
FAT 6g
SUGAR 2g

CALORIES
273

INGREDIENTS

- 1 MEDIUM YELLOW SQUASH
- 1 LB LEAN GROUND TURKEY
- KOSHER SALT
- GROUND BLACK PEPPER.
- 1 GREEN BELL PEPPER

FOR THE SAUCE
- TWO 8 OZ CANS, NO SALT ADDED, TOMATO SAUCE
- 1 TSP MINCED GARLIC
- ¼ YELLOW ONION DICED
- 2 BAY LEAVES

NOTES: *Spaghetti squash is nutritious low carb alternative to pasta. It's also rich in micronutrients such as vitamin B and C. In addition it has less calories than most pastas.*

This recipe can be made with the turkey meat sauce, or you can leave off the meat and use the red sauce alone. If you leave off the turkey, you could add in a scoop of protein powder to your recipe to get in some extra protein for the day. My preferred protein is *Devotion.* Their *Buttery Blend* flavor would work well in this recipe. You can also use a vegan protein for a healthy and tasty vegan version of this dish.

STEPS

1. Preheat the oven to 375 degrees. Wash the squash and place on a cutting board (lay it on a damp towel to prevent slipping). Cut the top and bottom ends off and cut it in half with a sharp chef's knife. Make sure to have your fingers out of the way.
2. Scoop out the seeds. Spray the inside of each half lightly with non-stick cooking spray, sprinkle on a little salt. Place on the pan skin side up. Roast the squash for 40-50 minutes. When you turn the halves over there should be browning on the edges and the strands of squash should pull up easily, to know it's done.
3. While the squash is cooking, spray a skillet and place on the stove on medium heat, add a little water and sauté the onion.
4. Add in the ground turkey to brown it, stirring as it cooks. Add in the chopped bell pepper, garlic, a pinch of salt and mix.
5. Stir in two cans of tomato sauce and the two bay leaves. Let simmer for five more minutes. (Use one or two cans of sauce-your preference).
6. You can use the squash shell to plate this dish. Pull up some of the squash strands to loosen it up. Add four to six ounces of the (meat) sauce. Enjoy!

DINNER RECIPE 6

Maple Glazed Chicken

PREP TIME: 10 MINUTES*

COOK TIME: 15 MINUTES

READY IN: 25 MINUTES

SERVINGS: 2 (8 OZ.)
MACROS:
CARBS 3g
PROTEIN 43g
FAT 3g
SUGAR 2g

CALORIES
230

INGREDIENTS

- 2 BONELESS SKINLESS CHICKEN BREASTS
- 2 TBS SUGAR FREE MAPLE SYRUP
- 1 TBS REDUCED SODIUM-SOY SAUCE
- 2 TSP LEMON JUICE
- 1 CLOVE MINCED GARLIC
- 1 TSP MINCED FRESH GINGER
- ¼ TSP FRESHLY GROUND BLACK PEPPER

NOTES: *This is a flavorful dish that is packed with protein. The maple glaze provides a tasty way to satisfy the sweeter side while the chicken provides a satiating meal.*

*Plan extra time for this dish. The chicken breasts will need to marinate in the glaze for at least two hours. You can prep this dish in the morning and leave it marinating for the day. When you are ready to eat it only will take 10 minutes to prepare and cook the food.

STEPS

1. Whisk syrup, soy sauce, lemon juice, garlic, ginger, and pepper in a small, shallow, dish. Wash the chicken breasts and add them to your dish. Turn them over a few times to coat them with the marinade. Cover the dish and set it inside the fridge for two hours. Turn over once during the marinating process.
2. Use an indoor or outdoor grill to cook the chicken. Spray the grill with cooking spray and then turn the heat to medium.
3. Remove the chicken from the marinade. Save the marinade, it will be made into a glaze. Cook the chicken on the grill for about 8 minutes per side. Internal temperature should be 165 degrees. (You can grill for less time and then place in the oven to bake at 350 degrees for 10 minutes).
4. While the chicken is cooking, pour the marinade into a small saucepan and bring to a simmer over medium heat. Cook until reduced by half. (Around four minutes).
5. Baste the chicken liberally with the glaze while it's cooking.
6. Remove the chicken from the grill or oven. turn off the heat. Enjoy!

   This dish can be served with a side of vegetables or rice (either white or brown) to get in some carbs. Remember to adjust your macros.

DINNER RECIPE 7 ★

 ## Healthy Stuffed Peppers

PREP TIME: 10 MINUTES

COOK TIME: 40 MINUTES

READY IN: 50 MINUTES

SERVINGS: 6 PEPPERS

MACROS: 2 PEPPERS WITH TURKEY

CARBS 12g

PROTEIN 32g

FAT 6g

SUGAR 2g

CALORIES: 170 PER PEPPER

INGREDIENTS

- 6 MEDIUM SIZE BELL PEPPERS
- ½ CUP FAST COOK JASMINE RICE
- 1 LB LEAN GROUND TURKEY OR LEAN BEEF.
- 1 YELLOW ONION CHOPPED
- 2 CLOVES GARLIC MINCED
- 2 8 OZ CANS TOMATO SAUCE (no salt added).
- 1 TBS WOCESTIRESHIRE SAUCE
- 1 TSP ITALIAN SEASONING
- ¼ CUP LOW FAT MOZARELLA CHEESE*
- SALT & PEPPER TO TASTE

NOTES: *Jasmine rice is a low fat, healthy source of carbs that's also filling! It provides a unique floral like taste to this recipe. You can substitute and use brown rice instead which provides more of an earthy taste.*

This recipe can be made with your preferred meat protein. Lean ground turkey, ground chicken, or lean ground beef, go well with the peppers.

For a vegan option, use chopped mushrooms and lentils for the protein.

Cheese topping is optional. Make sure to add it to your macros if you use it.

STEPS

1. Preheat the oven to 350 degrees.
2. Spray a large skillet with non-stick cooking spray and place it on the stove on medium heat. Add the onion and garlic, cook for three minutes. Add the ground turkey. Cook over medium until brown. Drain the fat from the meat (if needed).
3. While the meat is browning, cook the jasmine rice and set it aside.
4. Wash the peppers and cut off the tops. Scrape out the seeds and membrane.
5. Place a large pot of water on the stove, bring water to a boil, add a little salt to the water, add the peppers, boil for five minutes to soften them before baking.
6. Take the skillet with the browned meat, place back on the stove on low heat and **add one can of tomato sauce**, Worcestershire sauce, salt, and pepper to taste. Cook for five minutes more stirring a few times.
7. Spray a muffin pan with non-stick spray. Stand the peppers up in each well.
8. Fill each pepper with the ground meat mixture.
9. **Take the remaining can of tomato sauce**, pour in a small bowl, add the Italian seasoning. Stir to combine and pour a little over each pepper. Cover the peppers with foil and bake in the oven on the center rack for 35-40 minutes.
10. Remove from the oven. Turn off the heat. Uncover the foil and sprinkle one tsp. cheese on each pepper (optional). Serve immediately. Enjoy!

DINNER RECIPE 8
Healthy Orange Chicken

PREP TIME: 15 MINUTES

COOK TIME: 10 MINUTES

READY IN: 25 MINUTES

SERVINGS: 4

MACROS: (6 oz portion of chicken)

CARBS 6g
PROTEIN 26g
FAT 3g
SUGAR 2g

CALORIES: 160 PER SERVING

INGREDIENTS

- 1 LB CHICKEN BREAST, CUT INTO BITE SIZE PIECES
  MARINADE
- ½ TSP BAKING SODA
- KOSHER SALT TO TASTE
- 1 TBS FRESH ORANGE JUICE
- 1 ½ TBS SOY SAUCE (Low sodium variety).
- 1 TSP GROUND BLACK PEPPER
- 1 TBS CORNSTARCH
- 1 TSP GARLIC MINCED
- 1 TSP GINGER MINCED
  COOKING SAUCE
- 1 BOTTLE SUGAR FREE ORANGE GINGER MARINADE. (I prefer *G. Hughes* brand).
- ½ TBS CORNSTARCH
- 1 TBS MCT OIL

NOTES: *The original recipe for this dish called for a home-made marinade & cooking sauce. To save time, I made the 1st marinade from scratch and then used my favorite premade brand as the sauce to cook the chicken in. This cut back on the prep time, and it still turned out delicious!*

This recipe tastes just as delicious as the orange chicken you would get from your favorite Asian restaurant. The only difference is it's a healthier version with less fat and lower sodium.

For your carbs, this dish goes great on most types of rice. You can use jasmine, basmati, or even wild rice. Plan ½ cup per serving. Adjust your macros to include the rice you choose.

Optional garnishes: Sesame seeds, chopped green onion, and/or orange slices on the side.

STEPS

1. Rinse the chicken and cut it into bite size pieces. Take a large mixing bowl and mix all the ingredients for the marinade. Place the chicken in a ceramic dish and pour the marinade on top. Mix the chicken around until it is covered thoroughly. Cover the dish and place it in the fridge for 15 minutes to marinate.
2. Take a large skillet and place it on medium heat. Add the MCT oil until it melts. Add in the marinated chicken. Stir and cook the chicken evenly on both sides. Around five minutes per side.
3. Pour ½ the bottle of the *G. Hughes* sugar free marinade/sauce in a small bowl. Add the cornstarch and stir. Add it in to the cooked chicken to coat it and cook the chicken for five minutes more. Make sure to stir while cooking. The sauce should start to thicken and stick to the chicken nicely.
4. Remove the skillet from the heat and serve the chicken over rice. Enjoy!

MIDMORNING SNACK RECIPE 1

 ## Sinful Cinnamon Muffins

PREP TIME: 6 MINUTES

COOK TIME: 14 MINUTES

READY IN: 20 MINUTES

SERVINGS: 2 MUFFINS

CALORIES PER MUFFIN: 52

MACROS PER MUFFIN:

CARBS 3.3g
PROTEIN 4.9g
FAT 2.1g
SUGAR 1g

INGREDIENTS

- 30g (one scoop) *DEVOTION* PROTEIN *SINFUL CINNAMON FLAVOR
- ½ CUP PROTEIN PANCAKE MIX
- ½ TSP BAKING POWDER
- 1 ½ TSP CINNAMON
- ½ CUP WATER
- ¼ CUP UNSWEETENED APPLESAUCE
- ½ TSP VANILLA
- 1 PACK STEVIA® OR OTHER ARTIFICIAL SWEETENER (optional)

OPTIONAL TOPPINGS:

- SWERVE BROWN SUGAR
- CINNAMON

NOTES: *These delicious muffins are a great way to get in extra protein for the day, and they really satisfy that sweet craving. They can also be for breakfast. I like to have them post workout after my second meal of the day as a satiating snack.*

* **I use *Devotion* as my go to protein because it tastes great, contains whey protein isolate and micellar casein, plus digestive enzymes. It's also designed to be used for baking, so it's perfect for using in my recipes. You can find the link to *Devotion* on my website: Claremorrow.com under *My Favorites*. If you follow a vegan diet, you can use a vegan protein in this recipe. Make sure it is suitable for baking.**

STEPS

11. Preheat your oven to 375 degrees.
12. Take a six well muffin pan and line with baking cups or spray with pan spray.
13. Mix the dry ingredients in a medium bowl.
14. Mix the wet ingredients in a separate bowl.
15. Combine wet ingredients into the dry.
16. Pour the batter divided evenly into the six muffin wells.
17. Bake approximately 14 minutes.
18. Test with a toothpick to make sure the muffins are cooked through.
19. Take them out of the oven and turn off the heat.
20. Plate the muffins and top with some of the brown sugar & cinnamon. Enjoy!

MIDMORNING SNACK RECIPE 2 ★

Baked Oat Berry Cake

PREP TIME: 5 MINUTES

COOK TIME: 30-45 MINUTES

READ IN: 50 MINUTES

SERVINGS: 6-8 Slices

CALORIES TOTAL: 1,300

MACROS TOTAL CAKE:

CARBS 136g
PROTEIN 80g
FAT 25g
SUGAR 62g

INGREDIENTS

- 30g (one scoop) *DEVOTION* PROTEIN ANGEL FOOD CAKE*
- 3 MASHED RIPE BANANAS
- 2 CUPS FROZEN MIXED BERRIES OF CHOICE
- 2 CUPS STEEL CUT OATS
- 2 CUPS UNSWEETENED ALMOND MILK**
- ½ TSP CINNAMON
- 1/8 TSP SEA SALT

OPTIONAL TOPPING

- SUGAR FREE MAPLE SYRUP

NOTES: This is a delicious recipe that allows you to get in protein and carbs. It comes out as a denser cake, so it is filling. The berries provide a healthy source of micronutrients. Great recipe to prep with. Store in a sealed container in the fridge, to have in between meals during the week.

* I use *Devotion* as my go to protein because it tastes great, contains whey protein isolate and micellar casein, plus digestive enzymes. It's also designed to be used for baking, so it's perfect for using in my recipes. You can find the link to *Devotion* on my website: Claremorrow.com under *My Favorites*. If you follow a vegan diet, you can use a vegan protein in this recipe. Make sure it is suitable for baking. Vanilla flavor protein also works for this recipe.

STEPS

1. Preheat the oven to 350 degrees.
2. Spray a 9" ramekin with cooking spray (or use baking pan of choice for how thick you want the cake to be).
3. Place bananas on the bottom of the dish or pan and mash lightly with a fork.
4. Spread a layer of frozen berries on top of the bananas.
5. Mix the oats, cinnamon, and salt. Sprinkle the mix on top of the frozen fruit.
6. In a separate bowl mix the almond milk with the protein powder and pour it on top of the oats. Oat milk can be used instead of Almond milk**
7. Bake for 30-45 minutes until the bottom is golden.
8. Remove from the oven, turn off the heat.
9. Plate the cake and drizzle on some sugar free maple syrup. Enjoy!

MIDMORNING SNACK RECIPE 3
Blueberry Yogurt With an Egg

PREP TIME: 5 MINUTES

COOK TIME: 5 MINUTES

READY IN: 10 MINUTES

SERVINGS: 1

CALORIES YOGURT: 80

CALORIES BLUEBERRIES: 9

CALORIES WHOLE EGG: 72

MACROS:

YOGURT & BLUEBERRIES	1 WHOLE EGG
CARBS 16g	CARBS .06g
PROTEIN 20g	PROTEIN 6g
FAT 2g	FAT 5g
SUGAR 6g	SUGAR .02g

INGREDIENTS

- 5.3 OZ CONTAINER OF 0% GREEK YOGURT. (I prefer *Fage* brand). YOGURT OF CHOICE CAN BE USED AS LONG AS THE MACROS ARE SIMILAR.
- 10 BLUEBERRIES (Frozen or fresh).
- 1 WHOLE EGG*

OPTIONAL TOPPINGS
- CINNAMON
- HOT SAUCE

NOTES: *This snack is simple and nutritious! Snacks in between meals doesn't need to be complicated. Eating smaller portions of nutritious foods can prevent you from getting so hungry that you binge eat overprocessed, unhealthy, foods. Staying satiated using healthy choices, helps with fat loss goals.*

***Fat Loss Tip:** Did you know that most fruit flavored yogurt has added fruit juices that are high in sugar? For a healthier option, start with plain Greek yogurt and add in fresh fruit. Blueberries have less natural sugar than some other fruits like bananas or pineapple. Try to stick with adding berries to yogurt for a healthier option.

STEPS

1. Wash the fruit and add it to the Greek yogurt.
2. Sprinkle some cinnamon on top, if desired.
3. For the egg: Prepare one whole egg to your preference. A meal prep tip is to have hard-or soft-boiled eggs premade to make this snack easy to take with you when you are on the go.
4. *For less fat and calories, you can have one egg white instead of the whole egg. Adjust your macros in your food tracking app if you have just the egg white.
5. Salt and pepper to taste. Use pink Himalayan salt for a healthier salt seasoning.
6. For spicy flavor without calories add a dash of hot sauce on the egg. Enjoy!

MIDMORNING SNACK RECIPE 4

 Rice Cake with Toppings

PREP TIME: 10 MINUTES

COOK TIME: 0 MINUTES

READY IN: 10 MINUTES

SERVINGS: 2

MACROS:

1 RICE CAKE WITH YOGURT & STRAWBERRIES	1 RICE CAKE WITH PEANUT BUTTER & BROWNIE
CARBS 10g	CARBS 11g
PROTEIN 8g	PROTEIN 28g
FAT 1g	FAT 3g
SUGAR 2g	SUGAR 1g
CALORIES: 75	**CALORIES:** 191

INGREDIENTS

- 2 RICE CAKES (lightly salted or plain).
- 1 SCOOP CHOCOLATE PROTEIN* (I used *Devotion* Brownie Batter flavor).
- 2 WHOLE STRAWBERRIES
- 2 TBS PEANUT BUTTER POWDER (I prefer *PB 2* brand).
- 2 TBS 0 % GREEK YOGURT (I prefer *FAGE* brand).

OPTIONAL TOPPINGS

- SUGAR FREE MAPLE SYRUP
- PINCH OF SEA SALT

NOTES: *Rice cakes may seem boring, but they are a good source of carbs and it's easy to use them to make a quick, healthy, snack. The toppings listed here are suggestions. You can create your own rice cake recipe too! The goal with in between meal snacks is to get in some carbs and protein, while staying low on fat and avoiding added sugar as much as possible.*

* I use *Devotion* as my go to protein because it tastes great, contains whey protein isolate and micellar casein, plus digestive enzymes. It's also designed to be used for baking, so it's perfect for using in my recipes. You can find the link to *Devotion* on my website: Claremorrow.com under *My Favorites*. If you follow a vegan diet, you can use a vegan protein in this recipe.

STEPS

1. Remove the rice cakes from the packaging.
2. For the yogurt berry rice cake, rinse the strawberries and slice them. You can also use blueberries. Spread the 2 Tbs. of yogurt on the rice cake. Add the sliced strawberries. You can drizzle on some of the chocolate sauce or the sugar free maple syrup for extra flavor.
3. For the chocolate peanut butter rice cake take the PB Powder, mix two Tbs with one and ½ Tbs water. (You can adjust the water for your preferred consistency).
4. Take the scoop of brownie batter protein and mix it with ¼ cup water to make a sauce and spread that on the rice cake. Next do a layer of the PB sauce. Add a pinch of sea salt. Enjoy!

AFTERNOON SNACK RECIPE 1
Breadsticks with Dipping Sauce

PREP TIME: 10 MINUTES

COOK TIME: 10 MINUTES

READY IN: 20 MINUTES

SERVINGS: 1
MACROS: BREAD STICKS & SAUCE
CARBS 16g
PROTEIN 35g
FAT 3g
SUGAR 2g

CALORIES: 215

INGREDIENTS

FOR THE BREAD STICKS

- 1 SCOOP *DEVOTION* PROTEIN BUTTERY BLEND FLAVOR*
- ¼ CUP EGG WHITES. (TWO LARGE EGGS).
- GARLIC POWDER
- ITALIAN SEASONING
- 2 TBS FAT FREE MOZARELLA CHEESE.
- PINCH OF PINK SALT

FOR THE DIPPING SAUCE

- ONE 8 OZ CAN TOMATO SAUCE (No salt added).
- 2 TBS CHOPPED ONION
- ½ CLOVE MINCED GARLIC
- 1 BAY LEAF

NOTES: *These yummy breadsticks are a perfect late afternoon snack and really satisfy those bread cravings. They have less additives and calories found in most commercially made bread. The dipping sauce is a healthy source of vitamins. It provides the perfect bite to this savory recipe.*

* I use *Devotion* as my go to protein because it tastes great, contains whey protein isolate and micellar casein, plus digestive enzymes. It's also designed to be used for baking, so it's perfect for using in my recipes. You can find the link to *Devotion* on my website: Claremorrow.com under *My Favorite*s.

STEPS

1. Use a mini waffle maker for the bread sticks. Plug it in and turn the heat to medium. Spray the top and bottom grids with nonstick cooking spray.
2. Pour one scoop *Devotion* protein into a small bowl and add the egg whites. Mix well with a spoon. Add in a few dashes of garlic powder, Italian seasoning, and a pinch of salt.
3. Open the waffle maker and sprinkle one Tbs. cheese on the bottom grid. Pour the protein mix on and add another Tbs. of cheese. Close the waffle maker and let it cook for a few minutes until the batter is golden brown and cooked throughout.
4. Once the bread batter is done take it out from the waffle maker and use a pizza cutter to slice it into four bread sticks. Unplug the waffle maker.
5. Take a saucepan and spray it with non-stick cooking spray. Turn the stove to medium heat and add the onion and garlic, stir for 45 seconds. Add in the can of sauce and the bay leaf. Salt and pepper to taste. Let the sauce to simmer for eight to ten minutes.
6. Pour ½ cup dipping sauce in a bowl. Plate the bread sticks. Enjoy!

AFTERNOON SNACK RECIPE 2

Green Apple Caramel Nachos

PREP TIME: 10 MINUTES

COOK TIME: 2 MIUNTES

READY IN: 12 MINUTES

SERVINGS: 1

CALORIES: 165

MACROS: PER SERVING

CARBS 35g
PROTEIN 6g
FAT 4g
SUGAR 15g

INGREDIENTS

- 1 LARGE GREEN APPLE (I USE GRANNY SMITH)
- 1/8 CUP LILY'S SUGAR FREE DARK CHOLATE CHIPS
- 1/8 CUP *LILY'S* SUGAR FREE WHITE CHOCOLATE CHIPS

FOR THE CARAMEL SAUCE

- *1 TBS TOFFEE APPLE FLAVORED PEANUT POWDER (I USE *FLAVORED PB CO. BRAND*).

This recipe is fun to make and great for an occasional healthy snack in between meals. The combo of the crisp green apples with the caramel drizzle and the bits of chocolate and white chocolate makes this a tasty treat!

Although apples are a great source for getting in your daily micronutrients, they are higher in natural sugar. Because of that I stick to berries for most of my fruit choices for my diet.

For a lower calorie version of this recipe use jicama sticks in place of apples.

NOTES: *This recipe **uses a product that contains peanuts & dairy.** Avoid this recipe if you have peanut or dairy allergies or swap out the PB Powder for Walden Farms Sugar Free Caramel Dip. Then adjust the macros.*

STEPS

1. Wash the apple and cut out the core. Peeling is optional. Cut into even slices.
2. Place the chocolate chips into a food processor. Mix for only a few seconds to break the chips up into smaller pieces. Do not over process or the chips become powdery. Pour the chocolate chip crumbles into a small dish and set aside.
3. Pour the white chocolate chips into a microwave safe dish and heat just until melted. (You can also melt them on the stove in a pan).
4. Scoop out one Tbs. of the Toffee Apple Flavored PB Powder and place into a small bowl. Add one Tbs of water and mix it well until it makes a sauce.
5. Plate the apple slices on your dish. Drizzle with the caramel sauce and then drizzle on the warm white melted chocolate.
6. Sprinkle the chocolate chip crumbs on top. Enjoy!

AFTERNOON SNACK RECIPE 3
Spicy Tuna Quesadilla

PREP TIME: 10 MINUTES

COOK TIME: 5 MINUTES

READY IN: 15 MINUTES

SERVINGS: 1

MACROS:
CARBS 9g
PROTEIN 19g
FAT 2g
SUGAR 2g

5" Tuna Quesadilla, 1 Celery Stalk, ¼ Cup Ranch Dipping Sauce

CALORIES: 122

INGREDIENTS

- 2 LOW CARB TORTILLAS (I prefer *Mr. Tortilla* brand).
- ONE 2.6 OZ PACKET OF SPICY BUFFALO TUNA (I prefer *Starkist* brand)
- DASH OF RANCH SEASONING POWDER
- 1 STALK OF CELERY* (Optional).

FOR THE DIPPING SAUCES
- 2 TBS 0% GREEK YOGURT (I USE *FAGE* BRAND)
- 1 PACKET RANCH DRESSING/SEASONING MIX
- ½ CUP SALSA (Located in my sauces recipes).

NOTES: *Tuna is a great source of low calorie, protein This recipe uses the convenient, flavored, prepackaged tuna. You can make this recipe with any flavor pack you prefer. If you are making larger batches, it may be more economical to buy the tuna in cans. Make sure it's packaged in water, not oil. Mix it in a bowl with your favorite buffalo (or other flavored, sugar free) sauce. You can also use plain tuna.*

*Celery on the side is optional, but it does go perfectly with the ranch sauce (or salsa). Celery is a low-calorie snack, that has tons of health benefits. It can also be chopped up and added to the tuna before cooking.

STEPS

1. Open your waffle maker and spray the top and bottom with nonstick cooking spray. Plug it in and let it preheat.
2. Take one low carb tortilla and place it on the bottom of the waffle maker. I like to cook my bottom tortilla first for 45 seconds, so the inside gets cooked.
3. Open your packet of buffalo style tuna. Insert a spoon to scoop out the tuna onto the bottom tortilla. Place the second tortilla on top.
4. Close the waffle maker and let the quesadilla cook for around one minute more until it is golden brown.
5. Open the waffle maker, turn off the heat and plate your quesadilla. Use a pizza cutter to slice it into four wedges.
6. For the ranch dipping sauce: Spoon 2 Tbs Greek Yogurt in a small bowl, sprinkle in one to two tsp. of the ranch dressing mix into the yogurt. Stir until blended.
7. Wash your celery and cut it in half. Serve on the side of with the ranch sauce (and/or salsa) for dipping. Enjoy!

AFTERNOON SNACK RECIPE 4

Nacho Protein Pizza Bites

PREP TIME: 10 MINUTES

COOK TIME: 10 MINUTES

READY IN: 20 MINUTES

SERVINGS: 2

MACROS: 6 MINI PIZZAS

CARBS 18g
PROTEIN 24g
FAT 6g
SUGAR 2g

CALORIES: 260

INGREDIENTS

- ONE 8 OZ CAN TOMATO SAUCE (No salt added).
- ¼ CUP FAT FREE CHEESE (Pizza blend).
- *QUEST* PROTEIN CHIPS (Nacho cheese flavor).
- 1 MEDIUM TOMATO (Diced).
- ½ CUP SHREDDED LETTUCE
- 1 TBS ITALIAN SEASONING
- 1 TSP GARLIC POWDER

CLOUD BREAD CRUST

- 3 EGG WHITES & 1 YOLK
- 2 TBS 0% GREEK YOGURT (I prefer *FAGE* brand).
- ¼ TSP CREAM OF TARTAR
- 1/8 TSP KOSHER SALT

NOTES: These mini protein pizzas not only deliver a healthy bite, they're also fun to make! Great recipe to make with kids.

To assemble your pizzas: Preheat the oven to 350 degrees. Take your cloud bread and place it on a cutting board. Using a glass (diameter 4") cut out six circles on the cloud bread. Place your circles on a baking rack. In a bowl, mix the tomato sauce, Italian seasoning & garlic powder. Spread some sauce on each crust. Sprinkle a little of the cheese on top. Place in the oven for five minutes (just until the cheese melts). Pull the pan out of the oven. Sprinkle some lettuce and tomato on each pizza. Break up some of the *Quest* chips. (This recipe uses 1/4 of the bag). Sprinkle some on each pizza. Broil in the oven for around 45 seconds just to crisp up the chips. Enjoy!

STEPS FOR THE CLOUD BREAD CRUST

1. Preheat the oven to 300 degrees.
2. Separate the egg whites from the yolks.
3. Put the egg whites in a big bowl and add in the cream of tartar. Use an electric hand blender on high speed to whip them until stiff peaks form. (4-9 Minutes).
4. In a medium bowl combine **1 yolk,** the Greek Yogurt, and the salt.
5. Gently fold the yogurt-yolk mixture into the egg whites until it's an even color. Do **not** over mix.
6. Line a dark baking sheet with parchment paper and pour the mixture into a rectangle on your pan. Spread the batter until it is your desired thickness, then smooth out the batter with a spatula.
7. Bake on the middle rack for 30 minutes until golden brown.
8. Remove the pan from oven. Turn off the heat. Allow the bread to cool off. Enjoy!

SALAD RECIPE 1 ⭐⭐
Clare's Satiating Salad

PREP TIME: 10 MINUTES

COOK TIME: 0 MINUTES

READY IN: 10 MINUTES

SERVINGS: 1

MACROS:
CARBS 29g
PROTEIN 10g
FAT 6g
SUGAR 7g

CALORIES: 180

INGREDIENTS

FOR THE SALAD

- 1-2 CUPS LETTUCE. I USE SPRING MIX WITH SPINACH ADDED IN.
- 1 OZ SLICED ALMONDS
- 4 BLUEBERRIES
- 4 RASPERRIES
- 2 STRAWBERRIES
- 1 TBS. FETA CHEESE OR CRUMBLED BLUE CHEESE
- 1 MEDIUM TOMATO
- 1 SMALL CUMCUMBER
- ½ RICE CAKE (white cheddar flavor).

HONEY MUSTARD DRESSING

- 2 TBS YELLOW MUSTARD
- 1 TSP MONK FRUIT SUGAR
- ¼ CUP WATER

NOTES: Having a daily salad as part of your diet is one of the best ways to get in your daily requirement of micronutrients. Another great thing about salad is there really are no hard and fast rules limiting how much salad you eat. Where most people go wrong is by loading up on high calorie dressing! You also must be mindful of extras like nuts, dried fruit, and cheese. All those items can add up when it comes to fat and calories. I've included my low-calorie honey mustard dressing in this recipe. You can also use my low-calorie ranch dressing. The recipe is listed in sauces and dressings.

*Add chicken or shrimp to this salad to get a healthy source of protein in your diet. Make sure to add the extras to your macro calculations and enter them in your food tracking app.

STEPS

1. Place the lettuce in a strainer, rinse, and drain. Pour the lettuce into a bowl. Repeat the rinsing process with your berries. Cut your berries in half and trim the tops off the strawberries.
2. Rinse your tomato and cucumber and slice them (peeling is optional).
3. Mix your veggies in with the lettuce, top with the berries, the almond slivers, and the cheese. Salt and pepper to taste.
4. For the dressing, mix the yellow mustard, water, and monk fruit sugar in a salad dressing mixer bottle, shake until blended, pour some on your salad.
5. Crumble the rice cake on top of the salad for a delicious low-calorie crunch.

Heavy dressing adds a lot of calories to salad and masks the true flavor. Try eating a few salads without it and eventually you will notice a difference. Once that happens, you will not want to go back to dumping high calorie, fatty, dressings on your delicious salad.

SALAD RECIPE 2
BBQ Chicken With Broccoli Slaw

PREP TIME: 10 MINUTES

COOK TIME: 40 MINUTES*

READY IN: 50 MINUTES

SERVINGS: 1

MACROS:
CARBS 12g
PROTEIN 36g
FAT 6g
SUGAR 2g

CALORIES: 280

INGREDIENTS

FOR THE SLAW
- ½ CUP BROCCOLI SLAW
- 1 TBS SLIVERED ALMONDS

FOR THE CHICKEN
- 1 SMALL BREAST

FOR THE BBQ SAUCE
- SUGAR FREE BBQ SAUCE. (I use *G. Hughes* Brand).

FOR THE DRESSING
- 2 TBS GREEK YOGURT
- 1 TBS APPLE CIDER VINEGAR
- 1 TSP SUGAR FREE MAPLE SYRUP
- KOSHER SALT
- FRESH GROUND BLACK PEPPER

NOTES: Although slaw technically is not a salad, I've included it in this section since it can be used the same way you would use lettuce in a salad. Slaw is a great way to get a daily serving of vegetables in your diet and provides a crispy bite that goes well with most meat protein. It's also nice to have in the fridge to add to chicken and tuna wraps. **Fun fact: Broccoli slaw is made up of broccoli stalks, julienne carrots, and purple cabbage.**

*To save time when making this recipe, use the crock pot to slow cook the chicken. Place a few chicken breasts in the crock pot, turn it on to medium heat. Let the chicken slow cook for the day in their own juice (salt and pepper to taste). Add sugar free BBQ sauce the last hour of cook time. Mix it in well with the chicken You can store unused portions for meal prep. Using this method, the recipe will take the prep time only.

STEPS

1. Pre heat the oven to 350 degrees or warm up the grill.
2. Rinse the chicken off and pat it dry. Place the broccoli slaw in a strainer and rinse it with cold water.
3. Place the chicken in a bowl and add in ½ cup of BBQ sauce. Cover and let it stand for 10 minutes to marinate.
4. Bake the chicken in the oven on a pan covered in foil for 30-40 minutes or cook it on a grill coated with nonstick cooking spray. Baste the chicken with the BBQ sauce a few times while its cooking so it won't dry out.
5. Once the chicken is cooked set it aside to cool off. Slice the chicken into strips or cut it into 1" pieces.
6. Pour the broccoli slaw into a salad bowl and add the almonds.
7. Mix the ingredients for the dressing in a small bowl. Salt and pepper to taste.
8. Pour the dressing on the slaw and mix. Add the BBQ chicken. Enjoy!

SALAD RECIPE 3
Shrimp, Asparagus, and Avocado Salad

SERVINGS: 4
MACROS:

PREP TIME: 15 MINUTES
COOK TIME: 5 MINUTES
READY IN: 20 MINUTES

1 SERVING SALAD & DRESSING

CARBS 12g	CARBS 2g
PROTEIN 22g	PROTEIN 2g
FAT 9g	FAT 4g
SUGAR 2g	SUGAR 1g
CALORIES: 166	**CALORIES:** 27

INGREDIENTS

SALAD

- 4 CUPS BABY SPINACH
- ¼ CUP FRESH PARSLEY CHOPPED
- 20 SPEARS ASPARAGUS (1 BUNCH)
- 1 SMALL AVOCADO
- 3 GREEN ONIONS
- SALT & PEPPER TO TASTE

SHRIMP

- 1 LB. RAW SHRIMP PEELED AND DEVEINED

DRESSING

- LEMON VINAIGRETTE

NOTES: *This salad is perfect for the warmer weather. It consists mainly of green veggies which are such a great source of micronutrients. The shrimp adds a healthy source of protein and makes this a satiating meal. The lemon vinaigrette ties it all together for a delightful and zesty dish that is perfect to use for weekly prep or serve it family style.*

*FOR THE LEMON VINAIGRETTE: Mix in a jar, 1 tsp finely grated lemon zest, 2 Tbs. fresh squeezed lemon juice, 1 tsp. sugar free maple syrup, 1 tsp Dijon mustard, 1 garlic clove minced, ¼ tsp. salt, 1/8 tsp. fresh ground black pepper, 2 Tbs. water, 1 Tbs. MCT Oil.

Place the lid on the jar and shake the ingredients until blended (around 45 seconds). Vinaigrette can be stored in the fridge for up to 4 days.

STEPS

1. Bring both a medium pot of water and a medium sauté pan of water to a boil.
2. Add the shrimp to the pot and the asparagus to the pan. Cook both items for 2two to three minutes. Use tongs to transfer the shrimp and the asparagus to an ice water bath. Drain the asparagus and slice into 1 ½ inch pieces.
3. Rinse and drain the baby spinach and set aside. Slice the avocado in half and remove the seed. Score the insides of each half with a knife. Scoop out the avocado and set aside. Chop the green onion.
4. Take out a large salad bowl. Add the baby spinach, the shrimp, the asparagus, the avocado, the chopped green onion. Garnish with the parsley.
5. Season with salt and pepper to taste. Toss the salad a few times to mix.
6. Serve the salad with the lemon vinaigrette on the side. I like to pour some of the dressing from the jar into a salad dressing dispenser bottle and then place that on the table if serving family style. Enjoy!

SALAD RECIPE 4 ⭐
Mediterranean Tuna Salad

PREP TIME: 10 MINUTES

COOK TIME: 0 MINUTES

READY IN: 10 MINUTES

SERVINGS: 4

1 SERVING SALAD	2 TBS DRESSING
CARBS 11g	CARBS 4g
PROTEIN 16g	PROTEIN 2g
FAT 4g	FAT 4g
SUGAR 2g	SUGAR 2g
CALORIES: 120	**CALORIES: 40**

INGREDIENTS

FOR THE SALAD

- 2 CANS TUNA PACKED IN WATER
- 4 CUPS BUTTER LETTUCE
- ¼ CUP CHERRY TOMATOS (halved).
- ¼ CUP BLACK OLIVES (pitted).
- 2 TBS FETA (Or crumbled blue cheese).
- 1 TBS LEMON ZEST
- 1 SMALL RED ONION (thinly sliced).

FOR THE BALSAMIC DRESSING

- ¼ CUP BALSAMIC VINEGAR (Sugar free).
- 1-2 GARLIC CLOVES (Minced).
- 2 TBS FRESHLY SQUEEZED LEMON JUICE
- 1 TBS MCT OIL
- 1 TBS SUGAR FREE MAPLE SYRUP

NOTES: *Butter lettuce gives this salad a delicious way to get in a healthy serving of veggies. The combination of the tuna, olives, tomatoes, red onion, and feta or blue cheese crumble, along with the balsamic drizzled on top, pulls the whole dish together to make a satiating, delicious meal.*

Use this recipe to meal prep for the week or serve it family style. The red onions and olives can be substituted for other veggies of choice such as capers or bell pepper (yellow or red).

When serving salad I have my dressing on the side. This allows me to meal prep salad and add the dressing later to prevent it from getting soggy. The dressing on the side allows each person to use the amount of dressing they like, when serving family style.

STEPS

1. Place the lettuce in a strainer and rinse gently with cold water. Set to the side to dry. Zest one small lemon. Use the rest of the lemon for your dressing.
2. Wash the tomatoes and cut in half. Peel and slice the red onion.
3. Place all the veggies (halve the olives first) into a salad bowl and toss.
4. Open the cans of tuna and drain the water. Scoop the tuna on top of the salad and toss. Add the cheese crumble on top. Salt and pepper to taste.
5. For the dressing: In a small bowl, combine the balsamic vinegar, minced garlic (you can sub and use garlic powder), lemon juice, maple syrup, MCT oil.
6. Pour into a dressing mixing bottle. Shake well until combined. Enjoy!

SALAD RECIPE 5 ★ ★
Healthy Taco Salad

SERVINGS: 1

PREP TIME: 20 MINUTES
COOK TIME: 10 MINUTES
READY IN: 30 MINUTES

MACROS

WITH BEEF
CARBS 28g
PROTEIN 45g
FAT 10g
SUGAR 2g
CALORIES: 305

WITH TURKEY
CARBS 28g
PROTEIN 40g
FAT 12g
SUGAR 2g
CALORIES: 315

VEGAN RECIPE
CARBS 38g
PROTEIN 20g
FAT 14g
SUGAR 2g
CALORIES: 235

RANCH DRESSING
CARBS 2g
PROTEIN 3g
FAT 1g
SUGAR 1g
CALORIES: 16

INGREDIENTS

FOR THE SALAD

- 4 OZ COOKED LEAN GROUND BEEF, BISON, OR TURKEY
- 1 TBS TACO SEASONING
- 1 CUP CHOPPED ICEBURG LETTUCE
- 1 OZ RED KIDNEY BEANS
- ¼ CUP BLACK OLIVES
- 2 OZ LOW FAT PIZZA CHEESE
- ¼ CUP CHERRY TOMATOES
- ½ BAG *QUEST* PROTEIN CHIPS (Nacho cheese flavor).

FOR THE DRESSING

- 2 TBS 0% GREEK YOGURT
- 1 TBS RANCH SEASONING FROM THE PACKET.

NOTES: *Leaving out the taco shell bowl makes this salad a healthier version. The veggies listed can be substituted for any of your favorites. I've also included a vegan version that tastes delicious too! Topping this salad with some crushed up Quest Protein Chips gives it a fun aspect and adds a little more protein to your diet. Instead of sour cream, use my healthy low calorie yogurt ranch dressing.*

*For the vegan recipe: Replace the meat with ¼ cup chopped mushroom and ¼ cup lentils. Chop the mushrooms and sauté them lightly in a pan with a little nonstick spray on it. Cook the lentils and add them into the pan to cook with the mushrooms for one minute. Use cashew or almond cheese instead of the pizza cheese.

STEPS

1. Heat a skillet on the stove and spray with non-stick cooking spray. Add in the meat (or vegan protein) to the skillet and cook until brown. Add a little water while cooking if needed to prevent sticking. Remove pan from heat. Drain any liquids. Add in some of the taco seasoning mix. Cook for 40 seconds more.
2. Rinse the lettuce under cold water and set to the side to dry. Rinse the tomatoes. Cut the tomatoes and the olives in half.
3. Drain and rinse the kidney beans. Canned beans do not need to be cooked.
4. In a large salad bowl, add the lettuce and other veggies and toss. Add the meat (or vegan protein) on top. Crumble the *Quest* chips and sprinkle on the top.
5. Mix the yogurt and ranch seasoning in a small bowl to serve on top or the side. Garnish with slices of lime. Enjoy!

SALAD RECIPE 6 ★

Spicy Jicama Salad

PREP TIME: 10 MINUTES
COOK TIME: 0 MINUTES
READY IN: 10 MINUTES

SERVINGS: 4
MACROS PER SERVING:
CARBS 16g
PROTEIN 6g
FAT 2g
SUGAR 5g

CALORIES: 120

INGREDIENTS

FOR THE SALAD

- 1 MEDIUM JICAMA*
- ½ RED BELL PEPPER
- ½ YELLOW BELL PEPPER
- ½ GREEN BELL PEPPER
- ½ CUP CHOPPED RED ONION
- ½ MEDIUM CUCUMBER, SEEDED, & CHOPPED
- 1 SMALL NAVEL ORANGE, PEELED, SLICED CROSSWISE, ROUND OFF THE EDGES
- ½ CUP CHOPPED FRESH CILANTRO
- 1/3 CUP LIME JUICE
- PINCH CAYENNE PEPPER
- PINCH PAPRIKA
- SEA SALT (Finely Ground).

OPTIONAL

- ½ CUP AVOCADO
- 2 TBS EVOO

NOTES: Jicama is a vegetable grown in Mexico and central America. It has a crisp, slightly sweet taste like an apple. Jicama can be eaten raw or cooked. Mexican potato, Chinese turnip, and yam bean are all nicknames for Jicama. This is one of my favorite food swaps to use in salads (or as a snack). Jicama is packed with vitamins and other nutrients, with less sugar and calories than many other fruits.

*When you are shopping for jicama, choose ones that are small to medium size with unblemished skin. When preparing jicama, peel the skin like you would a potato. Wash the jicama and slice it into sticks that are about ½" thick. You can also purchase prepackaged jicama sticks which makes for easier meal prep.

If you are serving this salad as a side dish to a meal that has some fats included like chicken enchiladas, then the acidity of this dish without the avocado and extra virgin olive oil balances out the meal. If you are serving this salad alone, adding the avocado and oil balances out the dish itself. Just make sure to add those to your macros because they will increase the fat content and

STEPS

1. Wash the veggies. Peel and cut them up. Add them to a large salad bowl.
2. Add in the orange slices.
3. Toss the salad. Pour the lime juice all over it.
4. Sprinkle with a generous pinch of cayenne pepper and paprika.
5. Season with a good amount of salt (to taste).
6. Cover and let sit in the fridge for 30 minutes before serving. Enjoy!

SIDE DISH RECIPE 1 ⭐
Green Beans Almondine

PREP TIME: 10 MINUTES

COOK TIME: 15 MINUTES

READY IN: 25 MINUTES

SERVINGS: 4

MACROS PER SERVING:

CARBS 8g
PROTEIN 4g
FAT 7g
SUGAR 3g

CALORIES: 155

INGREDIENTS

FOR THE GREEN BEANS

- 1 LB HARICOTS VERTS (FRENCH GREEN BEANS)
- ½ CUP RAW SLICED ALMONDS
- 1 SHALLOT FINELY CHOPPED
- 2 CLOVES OF GARLIC MINCED
- ZEST OF 1 LEMON
- 2 TSP FRESH LEMON JUICE
- FRESHLY GROUND BLACK PEPPER
- KOSHER SALT

FOR THE ALMOND SAUTE

- 1 TBS MCT OIL OR AVOCADO OIL*

NOTES: Green beans are a great choice for a side dish. They are a healthy source of micronutrients while being more affordable than some other veggies. This recipe uses French green beans which are harvested earlier and thought to be slightly more flavorful. Regular green beans can be used too.

*Sauteing the almonds in MCT (or Avocado) oil brings out the smoky flavor which goes well with the green beans. If fat loss is a goal and the use of the oil adds too many calories to your diet for the day, you can sub out the oil with a low-calorie spray butter in the pan to sauté them in. Watch the almonds closely so they don't burn. Adjust the macros in this recipe to reflect subbing out the oil.

STEPS

1. Bring a large pot of salted water to a boil. Meanwhile, prep an ice bath by filing a large bowl with ice and water. Trim the ends off the green beans and boil them until crisp tender. For around 2-3 minutes. (You want them to be slightly undercooked because they will continue to cook more later). Use a slotted spoon to remove them from the hot water and immediately transfer to the ice bath for 3-4 minutes. Drain the green beans and set aside.
2. In a large skillet over medium-low heat, melt the MCT or Avocado oil right until it starts to bubble. Add the almonds, stirring frequently until golden brown. About 3-4 minutes. Add a few squirts of low cal. butter flavor spray while sautéing the almonds for more flavor.
3. Reduce the heat to low and add in the shallots and garlic. Cook for around 2-3 minutes more, stirring occasionally until fragrant.
4. Add in the green beans and mix well. Cook until the green beans are tender.
5. Stir in the lemon zest and juice. Toss to coat. Season with salt and pepper to taste. Remove from heat and serve in a large ceramic bowl. Enjoy!

SIDE DISH RECIPE 2 ⭐
Crispy Sweet Potato Fries

PREP TIME: 5 MINUTES*

COOK TIME: 20 MINUTES

READY IN: 25 MINUTES

SERVINGS: 1

MACROS: FRIES ONLY (NO SAUCE)

CARBS 27g

PROTEIN 3g

FAT 2g

SUGAR 6g

CALORIES: 135

INGREDIENTS

FOR THE FRIES

- 1 SWEET POTATO
- 2 CUPS COLD WATER
- 1 TBS CORN STARCH
- SEA SALT (FINELY GROUND)
- SMOKED PAPRIKA
- GARLIC POWDER
- BLACK PEPPER
- CHOPPED PARSLEY
- COOKING SPRAY (I use zero calorie *PAM* Olive Oil).

FOR THE DIPPING SAUCE (optional)

- SUGAR FREE KETCHUP OR BBQ SAUCE (I prefer *G. Hughes* Brand).

NOTES: *Sweet potatoes are a staple of my diet when fat loss is a goal. They are high in vitamins, a great source of fiber, and low in calories. Their sweet flavor can help curb sugar cravings, in a healthy way. Japanese yams are also a favorite of mine. They are even lower in calories. I use sweet potatoes when making fries because they have more moisture, so they won't dry out when cooking. Japanese yams are great to use in recipes when you cook them whole like a baked potato.*

*Cooking tips: The cold-water bath helps remove the starch from the potatoes. This helps them stay crisp when cooking. Wait until they are done to add salt because it can cause them to dry out when cooking. Cut the potato into same size slices so they bake evenly. Don't overcrowd the rack or pan to ensure they have air circulating around them when cooking.

STEPS

1. Wash the sweet potato and cut off the ends. Peeling is optional. Cut into even slices and place them in a cold-water bath for 30 minutes. *This can be done earlier in the day. Store your slices in a sealed container until ready to use.
2. Drain the sweet potato slices from the water, place them in a large plastic baggie. Spray a little bit of zero calorie oil into the bag, shake until slices are coated. Add in the corn starch. shake again until coated. Repeat with the seasonings. **(Wait to add the salt).**
3. **Air fryer cooking**: Place the slices in the basket, cook them on 380 degrees for around 20-25 minutes. Re spray them with the oil halfway through the cooking process.
4. **Oven cooking:** Preheat the oven to 400 degrees. Line a pan with parchment paper. Make sure the parchment paper is the kind that can be used with high heat. Spread the fries evenly on the pan.
5. Bake for 18-25 minutes. Make sure to flip them once during the baking process. Let them cool for five minutes on a wire rack. **Season with salt** and garnish with parsley. Enjoy!

SIDE DISH RECIPE 3

 Cauliflower Mashed Potatoes

PREP TIME: 10 MINUTES

COOK TIME: 20 MINUTES

READY IN: 30 MINUTES

SERVINGS: 1

MACROS:

CARBS 3g

PROTEIN 2g

FAT 6g

SUGAR 2g

CALORIES: 64

INGREDIENTS

FOR THE MASH

- 1 LARGE HEAD OF CAULIFLOWER BROKEN INTO FLORETS
- 1 TSP CRUSHED GARLIC
- 1 TBS ALMOND MILK
- 2 TBS VEGAN BUTTER
- SEA SALT
- FRESH GROUND BLACK PEPPER
- CHOPPED CHIVES (To garnish).

NOTES: Cauliflower is great to use as a side dish instead of using potatoes. It is a nutrient dense vegetable and a healthy source of fiber. Cauliflower has less calories and carbs than Potatoes. It is also thought to have anti-inflammatory and anti-aging properties.

*This recipe uses vegan butter which provides the creaminess for the mash while keeping this a vegan recipe. To lower the fat and calories, you can sub the vegan butter for pressed avocado oil. Adjust your macros to reflect the swap.

Cauliflower mash is a great way to sneak some healthy vegetables into your kids' diet. They won't even be able to tell it's not mash from potatoes.

STEPS

1. Soak the cauliflower head in a bowl of hot water with a pinch of salt to get the cauliflower extra clean.
2. Break the head into florets and steam it until it's very soft. **Steam is the best way to cook cauliflower for a mash**. Boiling it makes the cauliflower too watery.
3. Transfer the cauliflower into a deep bowl. Add in the garlic, almond milk, and butter. Mash the ingredients with a potato masher.
4. Use an immersion blender to mix the mash until it's smooth and creamy.
5. Add salt and pepper to taste.
6. Serve with chopped chives as a garnish. Salt and pepper to taste. Enjoy!

SIDE DISH RECIPE 4

Roasted Red Potatoes

PREP TIME: 10 MINUTES

COOK TIME: 35 MINUTES

READY IN: 45 MINUTES

SERVINGS: 6
MACROS PER SERVING:
CARBS 28g
PROTEIN 11g
FAT 8g
SUGAR 2g

CALORIES: 260

INGREDIENTS

- 1 ½ LBS BABY RED POTATOES* (If you can't find baby reds, you can use larger ones and cut them up).
- 2 TSP MINCED GARLIC
- ½ TSP BLACK PEPPER (Freshly ground).
- 1 TSP ITALIAN SEASONING
- ¼ CUP FINELY GRATED PARMESAN CHEESE
- OLIVE OIL SPRAY (Zero calorie).
- 1 TSP SEA SALT (Finely ground).
- 2 TABLESPOONS CHOPPED PARSLEY

NOTES: *Potatoes are one of my favorite foods for getting in healthy carbs for the day. Carbs are important when it comes to working out because they provide the fuel our body needs for energy and strength. When I work the larger muscle groups like back or legs, it's important to have the strength to get through my routine but also be able to push myself on some days with supersets or drop sets. Taxing muscles is how they grow over time. Healthy carbs as part of our diet are a key factor to being successful with fat loss and muscle growth.*

* Red potatoes are particularly healthy because of the thin, filled skins, which are loaded with fiber, vitamins, iron, and potassium. Half of the fiber of a potato comes from the skin. On red potatoes in particular, the skin is already super thin, so it doesn't detract from the taste or texture.

If fat loss is a goal, you can use less parmesan cheese or omit it altogether. That cuts the calories by 90g, the fat by 6g, the protein by 9g.

STEPS

1. Preheat the oven to 400 degrees. Line a sheet pan with foil and spray with a little of the olive oil cooking spray.
2. Wash the potatoes and cut them in half.
3. Add the potatoes to a large bowl. Lightly spray them with the olive oil. Stir them to coat with the oil. In a small bowl add the minced garlic, pepper, Italian seasoning, parmesan cheese, and salt. Mix and add it to the potatoes. Toss to coat.
4. Place the potatoes on the foil lined pan in a single layer.
5. Bake 35-40 minutes until golden brown or fork tender. Remove from the oven and turn off the heat.
6. Place them in a bowl to serve family style. Garnish with parsley flakes. Enjoy!

SAUCES, DIPS, & DRESSINGS 1 ★

 ## Homemade Red Sauce

PREP TIME: 5 MINUTES

COOK TIME: 10 MINUTES

READY IN: 15 MINUTES

SERVINGS: MAKES 8 OUNCES

MACROS:

CARBS 8g
PROTEIN 2g
FAT 1g
SUGAR 3g

CALORIES: 25

INGREDIENTS

- 8 OZ CAN TOMATO SAUCE (No salt added).
- 2 TBS CHOPPED ONION
- ½ CLOVE MINCED GARLIC
- 1 BAY LEAF
- KOSHER SALT
- BLACK PEPPER (Freshly ground).

NOTES: Most commercially sold pasta sauces have added sugar and they are high in potassium. Taking time to make your own sauce can help you cut back on the calories in your diet. Plus your homemade sauce will taste better!

This easy to make red sauce is great to use on pizza and pasta. It's also great to use as a dipping sauce for bread sticks.

STEPS

1. Spray a sauce pan with non-stick cooking spray. Turn the stove top to medium heat. Place the pan on the stove top.
2. Add the chopped onion and minced garlic to the saucepan. Sauté for 60 seconds on medium low heat.
3. Add in the can of sauce and bay leaf.
4. Let the sauce to simmer for 8-10 minutes on low. Salt and pepper to taste.
5. Remove the sauce from the stove. Turn off the heat.
6. Pour the red sauce into a ceramic ramekin to cool off. Enjoy!

You can store any unused sauce in a sealed container in the fridge for two days. To reheat the sauce, pour it into a ceramic dish and cover with a damp paper towel, and microwave on low for 30 seconds. You can also reheat the sauce on medium heat in a pan on the stove.

SAUSES, DIPS, & DRESSINGS 2 ★

Homemade Salsa

PREP TIME: 15 MINUTES

COOK TIME: 0 MINUTES

READY IN: 15 MINUTES

SERVINGS: MAKES 6 OUNCES SALSA

MACROS FOR 6 OUNCES:
CARBS 9g
PROTEIN 3g
FAT 2g
SUGAR 6g

CALORIES: 65

INGREDIENTS

- 2 MEDIUM TOMATOS
- 1 GARLIC CLOVE MINCED
- 1 LIME
- 1 TSP CILANTRO (Optional)
- ½ JALAPENO CHOPPED
- ¼ ONION CHOPPED
- SEA SALT (FINELY GROUND)
- BLACK PEPPER (FRESHLY GROUND)
- 1/8 TSP CUMIN

NOTES: There is 80 calories and 16 grams of sugar in ¼ cup of most ketchup brands! Once I started working with a bodybuilding coach, I was surprised to learn how many "unsuspecting" calories can sneak into our diets through condiments like ketchup and mayonnaise. Learning how to swap those out for healthier choices like salsa and yogurt ranch dip, really made a difference when it came to trying to get rid of the last bit of belly fat and achieve my fat loss goals.

This recipe makes 6 oz. salsa. My portion size is 2-3 ounces per serving. Make sure to adjust the macros in your food tracking app for your serving size.

*Not only is salsa a healthy swap for ketchup on things like burgers, but it can also make a great in between meal or snack when you have it with something else that's healthy like celery, cucumber, or protein chips. I love salsa with the *Quest* protein chips Chili Lime flavor. My homemade salsa recipe has a lot less sodium too!

STEPS

1. Wash the tomatoes and cut them up into smaller pieces.
2. Mince the garlic glove. Peel the onion and dice. Rinse and chop the jalapeño.
3. Cut the lime in half so you can use the juice in the salsa.
4. Take out a food processor or blender and add the tomatoes and other chopped veggies into the mixer and pulse on low speed until ingredients are just blended.
5. Squeeze in the lime juice and add in the cilantro and cumin.
6. Pulse the salsa again until it's the thickness you prefer. Add salt and pepper to taste. Mix again for just a few seconds.
7. Pour the salsa into a ceramic dish. Let it rest for five minutes and serve.
8. You can store unused portions in a sealed container in the fridge for five days. Enjoy!

SAUCES, DIPS, & DRESSINGS 3 ★
Tastes Like Honey Mustard

PREP TIME: 5 MINUTES

COOK TIME: 0 MINUTES

READY IN: 5 MINUTES

SERVINGS: 4 OUNCES

Dressing   **Dipping Sauce**

MACROS:

	DRESSING	DIPPING SAUCE
CARBS	0g	2g
PROTEIN	0g	0g
FAT	0g	0g
SUGAR	0g	2g
	0 Calories	4 Calories

INGREDIENTS

FOR THE DRESSING

- 4 OZ YELLOW MUSTARD (I prefer *French's* brand).
- 1 TBS MONK FRUIT SUGAR (I prefer *Purisure* brand)
- 2 TBS WATER
- BLACK PEPPER (Freshly ground).

FOR THE DIPPING SAUCE

- 4 OZ YELLOW MUSTARD (I prefer *French's* brand).
- 1 TBS SUGAR FREE MAPLE SYRUP

NOTES: Part of being able to maintain a healthy diet and stay within a calorie deficit when fat loss is a goal, is using food swaps. Rather than cutting out salad dressings and flavorful dipping sauces from my diet I substitute homemade low-calorie recipes instead. Denying ourselves our favorite foods to lose weight is not only difficult to do, but it can lead to binge eating. Instead look for healthy options that still satisfy certain cravings in a way that includes less fat, less added sugars, and less calories.

*The key to these recipes is to use a mustard that has zero calories. It may be tempting to try a Dijon mustard for example, but that contains white wine, and that means more added sugar and higher calories.

For the monk fruit sugar, I like *Purisure* brand because it doesn't contain sugar alcohols which can cause bloating.

STEPS

1. **For the dressing:** In a salad dressing container mix four ounces yellow mustard, one Tbs Monk Fruit sugar, two Tbs water (you can use less for thicker dressing), black pepper to taste.
2. Shake the dressing bottle until the ingredients are well blended.
3. Serve on the side with the salad. Enjoy!

For the dipping sauce: In a ramekin dish, mix four ounces yellow mustard and one Tbs sugar free maple syrup. Mix with a spoon until well blended. Enjoy!

The dipping sauce goes great with foods like chicken strips or pretzels. It's also great to use as a sauce on turkey, chicken, or vegan wraps.

SAUCES, DIPS, & DRESSINGS 4

Healthier Ranch

PREP TIME: 5 MINUTES

COOK TIME: 0 MINUTES

READY IN: 5 MINUTES

SERVINGS: 4 OUNCES

Dressing   Dipping Sauce

MACROS:

DRESSING	DIPPING SAUCE
CARBS 5g	CARBS 3g
PROTEIN 9g	PROTEIN 9g
FAT 2g	FAT 0g
SUGAR 2g	SUGAR 0g
65 Calories	45 Calories

INGREDIENTS

FOR THE DRESSING

- 4 OZ GREEK YOGURT 0% (I prefer *FAGE* brand).
- 1 TBS RANCH SEASONING (I prefer *Hidden Valley* Brand).
- 1 TSP FRESH SQUEEZED LEMON JUICE
- 1 TBS UNSWEETENED COCONUT MILK

FOR THE DIPPING SAUCE

- 4 OZ GREEK YOGURT 0% (I prefer F*AGE* brand).
- 1 TBS RANCH SEASONING (I prefer *Hidden Valley* BRAND).

NOTES: Part of being able to maintain a healthy diet and stay within a calorie deficit when fat loss is a goal, is using food swaps. Rather than cutting out salad dressings and flavorful dipping sauces from my diet, I substitute homemade low-calorie recipes instead. Denying ourselves our favorite foods to lose weight is not only difficult to do, but it can lead to binge eating. Instead look for healthy options that still satisfy certain cravings, just in a way that includes less fat, less added sugars, and less calories.

*This recipe uses low fat 0% Greek Yogurt as the base ingredient. When you combine the ranch seasoning with the yogurt, the flavor and texture is almost identical to commercially made ranch dressing which has 72 calories and 15g of fat per Tbs! Try using the dipping sauce for any of your raw veggies. It goes great with cucumbers, celery, and broccoli. I try to limit carrots in my diet since they have more natural sugars than the others I listed.

STEPS

1. **For the dressing:** In a tall bottle add 4 ounces Greek Yogurt, 1 Tbs Ranch Seasoning, 1 tsp lemon juice, 1 Tbs unsweetened coconut milk.
2. Use a hand immersion blender to blend/whip the ingredients. For thinner dressing add a little more coconut milk.
3. Pour the mixture into a dressing bottle. Shake to blend before pouring.
4. Serve on the side with the salad. Enjoy!

For the dipping sauce: In a ramekin dish mix 4 ounces Greek yogurt and 1 Tbs ranch seasoning. Mix with a spoon until well blended. Enjoy!

SAUSES, DIPS, & DRESSINGS 5 ★

Lo Cal Peanut Butter Syrup

PREP TIME: 5 MINUTES
COOK TIME: 0 MINUTES
READY IN: 5 MINUTES

SERVINGS: 1
MACROS:
CARBS 7g
PROTEIN 5g
FAT 1.5g
SUGAR 3g

CALORIES 49

INGREDIENTS

- 2 TBS PEANUT BUTTER POWDER (I prefer *PB2* brand).
- 1 ½ TBS WATER
- 2 OUNCES (4 TBS) MAPLE SYRUP (Sugar free).

OPTIONAL*
- ½ TSP VANILLA EXTRACT
- 1/8 TSP KOSHER SALT

NOTES: Peanut Butter is a controversial diet food! You will often hear fitness influencers talking about peanut butter as part of their diet since it is a nutrient dense food. Unfortunately most store-bought brands are very high in fat and calories. **One of the most popular peanut butter brands contains 95 calories and 8g of fat, in 1 Tbs!** Then there's the problem of "who can stop at just one serving?" 1 Tbs leads to two which leads to three. Lol!

Instead of cutting peanut butter completely out of my diet when trying to stay in a calorie deficit I learned how to food swap for something that satisfies my PB craving but with much less fat and calories. PB powder is a healthy source of protein, but it's a much better choice when fat loss is a goal.

*This recipe is easy to make and can be adjusted to suit your tastes. You can add more water if you like a thinner syrup or less if you like it thicker. Great to use on crepes, rice cakes, and protein pancakes. You can even sprinkle a few *Lily's* sugar free chocolate chips on top or the syrup for a yummy bite that satisfies sweet cravings in a healthier way.

STEPS

1. In a small bowl, combine the PB powder and water. Mix until well blended.
2. Add in the maple syrup. Mix well again until blended.
3. Serve the syrup in a bowl with a small spoon or in a creamer type bottle to drizzle it on. Enjoy!

OPTIONAL: For more of a caramel flavored syrup add the vanilla extract and salt after step two and mix well. * Add six calories to your macros with this option.

SAUCES, DIPS, & DRESSINGS 6

Chocolate & PB Dipping Sauces

PREP TIME: 5 MINUTES

COOK TIME: 0 MINUTES

READY IN: 5 MINUTES

SERVINGS: 1

Chocolate Sauce

Chocolate & PB Sauce

MACROS FOR THE SAUCES:

	CHOCOLATE	PEANUT BUTTER
CARBS	4g	5g
PROTEIN	20g	5g
FAT	2g	1.5g
SUGAR	0g	1g
Calories	110	45

INGREDIENTS

FOR THE CHOCOLATE SAUCE

- 1 SCOOP CHOCOLATE PROTEIN POWDER (I prefer *Devotion* brand * I used Brownie Batter flavor).
- 4 TBS (¼ cup) WATER

FOR THE PEANUT BUTTER SAUCE

- 1 TBS PEANUT BUTTER POWDER (I prefer *PB 2* brand)
- 1 ½ TBS WATER

NOTES: *If the thought of cutting chocolate out of your diet has you avoiding any type of weight loss plan, you're in luck! I used to think that being in a calorie deficit meant saying goodbye to any type of chocolatey goodness. Part of being successful on my Fluffy to Fit journey was learning how to incorporate foods that I loved into my diet in a healthier way. These two sauces are an example of using healthier ingredients to make delicious desserts and snacks that satisfy my sweet cravings without all the fat and calories.*

* I use *Devotion* as my go to protein because it tastes great, contains whey protein isolate and micellar casein, plus digestive enzymes. It's also designed to be used for baking, so it's perfect for using in my recipes. You can find the link to *Devotion* on my website: Claremorrow.com under *My Favorites*. If you follow a vegan diet, you can use a vegan protein in this recipe. Make sure it is suitable for baking.

STEPS

- **For the chocolate sauce:** In a small bowl, combine the protein powder with the water. Stir until well blended. You can adjust the amount of water in the recipe for the thickness you prefer.
- **For the peanut butter sauce:** In a small bowl, mix the PB powder with the water. Stir until well blended. Enjoy!

These sauces are great to use alone or swirl them together for a chocolate peanut butter combo. Strawberries dipped in the chocolate is one of my favorites for an in between meal snack. The chocolate peanut butter swirl is great to add to overnight oats.

DESSERT RECIPE 1
Watermelon Fruit Pizza

PREP TIME: 10 MINUTES

COOK TIME: 0 MINUTES

READY IN: 10 MINUTES

SERVINGS: 4

MACROS: PER SERVING

CARBS 11g

PROTEIN 2g

FAT 1g

SUGAR 8g

CALORIES: 53 Per Serving

INGREDIENTS

- 1 MEDIUM SIZE RIPE WATERMELON. CUT OFF A 1 ½" THICK SLICE (approx. 8" diameter).
- 4 TBS GREEK YOGURT 0% (I prefer *FAGE* brand).
- 2 TBS MAPLE SYRUP (sugar free).
- 4 MEDIUM STRAWBERRIES
- 2 TBS BLUEBERRIES
- ¼ CUP BLACKBERRIES
- 1 KIWI*
- 4 FRESH MINT LEAVES (Or ¼ tsp. dried flakes)

NOTES: When it comes to fruit as part of my daily diet, I try to stick to berries as much as possible because they have less sugar than other fruits such as watermelon and kiwi. For this recipe, I use the watermelon as a faux crust for a delicious dessert that is perfect on a hot summer day and the kiwi mimics pepperoni. Recipes like this are fine to make occasionally as a treat. To meet your daily dose of micronutrients (and if fat loss is a goal), stick with

*If Kiwis are out of season or you cannot find them locally you can leave it off and increase the blackberries to ½ cup.

You can use fresh or frozen berries for this recipe. Rinse the fruit gently under warm water to defrost.

STEPS

1. Slice off the end of the watermelon. Cut a 1 ½" thick slice that is a circle shape. For this recipe the watermelon "crust" had an 8" diameter.
2. In a bowl, mix the yogurt with the maple syrup. Spread it out in an even layer on the watermelon crust like spreading red sauce on pizza.
3. Wash the fruit and slice it to the size pieces you like for your toppings.
4. Wash the mint leaves (if using fresh). Sprinkle the mint on as a garnish that mimics red pepper flakes.
5. Cut the watermelon fruit pizza into four slices. Serve immediately. Enjoy!

For this recipe, I used one medium size ripe watermelon. You can slice your whole watermelon into 1 ½ circles to make multiple "pizzas" for guests or family. This is a fun recipe for kids to make and a great way to get healthy nutrients in their diet.

DESSERT RECIPE 2

Chocolate PB Rice Krispie Bars

PREP TIME: 10 MINUTES

COOK TIME: 5 MINUTES

READY IN: 15 MINUTES

SERVINGS: 6

MACROS PER BAR

CARBS 18g

PROTEIN 2g

FAT 7g

SUGAR 1g

CALORIES: 102

INGREDIENTS

- 2 PLAIN RICE CAKES
- 1 CUP SUGAR FREE CHOCOLATE CHIPS (I prefer *LILY'S* brand).
- 2 TBS PEANUT BUTTER POWDER* (I prefer *PB FIT* brand).
- 2 TBS MAPLE SYRUP (sugar free).
- ¼ TSP SEA SALT

NOTES: *Being in a calorie deficit to lose fat doesn't mean you can't sneak in some guilty pleasures. The key is learning how to swap unhealthy ingredients (found in most prepackaged desserts) for healthier ones. These homemade Rice Krispie bars are a great example of a healthier version that still satisfies sweet cravings.*

Store bought Rice Krispie treats have 130 calories per bar. Most of that is from the 12 grams of added sugar per treat! With these homemade bars you can reduce the calories and the sugar, and they taste better. These bars are fun to make with kids for an in between meal snack. They can be stored in a sealed container in the fridge for up to five days and are great to pack as an on-the-go snack.

*The PB powder is optional. These bars can be made with just the chocolate chips. Adjust the macros in the recipe if needed.

STEPS

1. Crumble two plain rice cakes in a bowl. Drizzle in the maple syrup and mix gently with a spoon to combine and make sticky rice.
2. Pour the chocolate chips (except two Tbs) in a saucepan and melt them on low heat. Stir in the salt.
3. In a small bowl mix the PB Powder with 1 ½ scoop of water.
4. Stir the melted chocolate into the crumbled rice cakes.
5. Take a 9" x 9" baking pan and line with parchment paper.
6. Pour the chocolate coated rice crispies into the pan. Use a spatula to spread them out, but do not flatten yet.
7. Use a spoon to drizzle on the PB allowing some to drip in the cracks.
8. Use the spatula to flatten the mixture. Sprinkle on the two Tbs of chocolate chips. Press on them slightly so they stick to the treats.
9. Place the pan in the fridge for at least 30 minutes before serving. Cut the rice treats into bars. Enjoy!

DESSERT RECIPE 3
Protein Carrot Cake

PREP TIME: 10 MINUTES

COOK TIME: 2 MINUTES*

READY IN: 12-15 MINUTES

SERVINGS: 4

MACROS PER SLICE

CARBS 9g
PROTEIN 10g
FAT 5g
SUGAR 5g

CALORIES: 110

INGREDIENTS

FOR THE CAKE

- 1 LARGE CARROT SHREDDED (approx. ¼ cup).
- 1 SCOOP PROTEIN POWDER** (I prefer *Devotion* Sinful Cinnamon flavor).
- 1 WHOLE EGG
- ¼ CUP SUGAR FREE APPLESAUCE
- 1 TBS CHOPPED WALNUTS
- 1 OUNCE RAISINS
- ½ TSP CINNAMON
- ¼ TSP NUTMEG

FOR THE ICING

- 1 ½ TBS FAT FREE CREAM CHEESE
- ½ SCOOP PROTEIN POWDER* (I prefer *Devotion* Angel Food Cake flavor).
- ¼ CUP WATER
- 2 TBS SHREDDED COCONUT*

NOTES: *This carrot cake recipe is packed with protein and is so easy to make. I like to cook mine in the microwave.* ***You can also try baking it in the oven at 350 degrees in for 8-10 minutes.*** *I did not include the shredded coconut in the macros. If you add that to the frosting, make sure to adjust your macros. This cake is great to meal prep with. Pack it with your meal for a delicious and nutritious dessert*

** I use *Devotion* as my go to protein because it tastes great, contains whey protein isolate and micellar casein, plus digestive enzymes. It's also designed to be used for baking, so it's perfect for using in my recipes. You can find the link to *Devotion* on my website: Claremorrow.com under *My Favorites*. If you follow a vegan diet, you can use a vegan protein in this recipe. Make sure it is suitable

STEPS

1. Spray a microwave safe baking dish with non-stick cooking spray.
2. Add in the carrots, egg, Sinful Cinnamon protein, applesauce, walnuts, raisins, cinnamon, and nutmeg. Mix with a spoon until it's well blended.
3. Place the dish in the microwave and cook for 60-90 seconds. (Do not overcook or you cake will be dry). If you are using an oven, mix the ingredients and pour the batter into an 8" round cake pan sprayed with non-stick cooking spray.
4. Once the cake comes out of the microwave (or oven) flip it upside down onto a plate.
5. Mix the Angel Food Cake protein with a little water and blend it with the cream cheese in the bowl.
6. Spread the frosting on the cake once it has cooled off. Sprinkle on the coconut. Enjoy!

DESSERT RECIPE 4

 ## *Ooey Gooey Fudge Brownies*

PREP TIME: 5 MINUTES

COOK TIME: 35 MINUTES

READY IN: 40 MINUTES

SERVINGS: 1 BROWNIE

MACROS:
CARBS 14g
PROTEIN 5g
FAT 1.5g
SUGAR 2g

CALORIES: 90

INGREDIENTS

- ½ CUP EGG WHITES
- 2 SCOOPS PROTEIN POWDER* (I prefer *Devotion* Brownie Batter flavor).
- 3 OVERRIPE BANANAS
- ½ CUP COCOA POWDER
- 2 CUPS OLD FASHIONED OATS
- ¼ CUP *SWERVE* (brown sugar substitute).
- 1 TSP VANILLA EXTRACT
- 1 CUP ALMOND MILK
- ¼ CUP SUGAR FREE CHOCOLATE CHIPS (I prefer *LILY'S* brand).

NOTES: *Recipes like this are what helped me stay on track with my fat loss goals. Instead of denying myself occasional chocolatey desserts (which only tempted me to binge eat when I finally gave in), I learned how to sub out ingredients that are high in fat and calories for healthier options. Who says you can't have your brownies and eat them too? Lol!*

* I use *Devotion* as my go to protein because it tastes great, contains whey protein isolate and micellar casein, plus digestive enzymes. It's also designed to be used for baking, so it's perfect for using in my recipes. You can find the link to *Devotion* on my website: Claremorrow.com under *My Favorites*. If you follow a vegan diet, you can use a vegan protein in this recipe. Make sure it is suitable for baking.

STEPS

1. Preheat the oven to 350 degrees.
2. Add all the ingredients listed (except for the chocolate chips) into a blender. You can also add them to a large mixing bowl and mix with a hand blender. Mix or blend the ingredients until well combined.
3. Take a 9" x 9" baking pan and lightly spray the bottom and sides with non-stick cooking spray.
4. Pour the brownie batter into the pan.
5. Add in half the ¼ cup chocolate chips and mix in with a spoon.
6. Place the pan on the center rack of the oven and cook for 35 minutes. Check the brownies with a toothpick in the middle after 30 minutes. Do not overcook or the batter will be dry.
7. Turn off the heat and take the brownies out of the over. Sprinkle the rest of the chocolate chips on top of the brownies once they cool off for 10 minutes.
8. Slice the brownies into 10 pieces. Enjoy!

DESSERT RECIPE 5 ⭐

 ## Mango Pineapple Nice Cream

PREP TIME: 5 MINUTES

COOK TIME: 5 MINUTES

READY IN: 10 MINUTES

SERVINGS: 6

MACROS PER SERVING

CARBS 12g

PROTEIN 1g

FAT 0g

SUGAR 8g

CALORIES: 55

INGREDIENTS

- 1 16 OZ PACKAGE OF FROZEN PINEAPPLE CHUNKS
- 1 CUP FROZEN MANGO CHUNKS* (OR 1 MEDIUM SIZE MANGO SEEDED, PEELED, AND DICED).
- 1/8 TSP KOSHER SALT
- 1 TBS LEMON OR LIME JUICE

NOTES: *If you love ice cream as much as I do but the thought of all the dairy, fat, and high calories found in most ice cream brands has you going without, this recipe is for you! This recipe makes a light and creamy ice cream like dessert without the high calories and fat. It's also dairy-free, egg free, and diabetes appropriate. Another bonus is that it is a tasty dessert to serve to anyone on a vegan diet.*

If you have issues with bloating after you eat dairy, you are not alone. The problem is that most commercially sold dairy products including cheese and milk are very over processed. In addition our digestive system can slow down as we age due to not moving around as much. This only compounds the problem. I try to avoid most dairy products, or I find recipes like this one so I can satisfy my ice cream cravings without all the bloating and high calories from cream or milk. I also take digestive enzymes as a daily supplement. You can find the ones I use in my *Amazon* store located on my website: Claremorrow.com.

STEPS

1. In a food processor add the pineapple and the mango. *If you use frozen mango you may need to add ¼ cup water. Blend until combined.
2. Add in the lemon (or lime) juice and the salt.
3. Blend until smooth and creamy.
4. Pour into ceramic bowls.
5. Serve immediately. Enjoy!

To add a little "zing" to the dish, sprinkle a little Tajin seasoning on the ice cream.

DESSERT RECIPE 6

Chocolate & Peanut Butter Protein Oat Balls

PREP TIME: 10 MINUTES

FRIDGE TIME: 30 MINUTES

READY IN: 40 MINUTES

SERVINGS: 8

MACROS PER BALL:

CARBS 18g

PROTEIN 14g

FAT 5g

SUGAR 2g

CALORIES: 153

INGREDIENTS

- 1 ½ CUPS OLD FASHIONED OATS
- 3 SCOOPS PROTEIN POWDER* (I prefer *Devotion* Angel Food Cake Flavor).
- 2 OZ SUGAR FREE CHOCOLATE CHIPS (I prefer *LILY'S* brand).
- 1/3 CUP PEANUT BUTTER POWDER (I prefer *PB FIT* brand).
- 1/4 CUP WATER
- 2 TBS MAPLE SYRUP (sugar free).

NOTES: *These protein balls make a great in between meal snack. Not only do they satisfy sweet cravings, but they also provide a healthy way to get in some extra protein for the day. I like to make them in larger batches and store them in the fridge for the week. They come in handy to pack with my meals for when I am out for the day or traveling. Meal prep is one of the best ways to ensure you stay within a calorie deficit when fat loss is a goal. It also can prevent you from resorting to grabbing unhealthy, high calorie snacks, when you are on the go.*

*I use *Devotion* as my go to protein because it tastes great, contains whey protein isolate and micellar casein, plus digestive enzymes. It's also designed to be used for baking, so it's perfect for using in my recipes. You can find the link to *Devotion* on my website: Claremorrow.com under *My Favorites*. If you follow a vegan diet, you can use a vegan protein in this recipe.

STEPS

1. In a bowl, combine oats, protein, peanut butter powder, water, and maple syrup.
2. Mix the batter with a spoon, or your hands, until combined.
3. Melt the chocolate chips in a pan, on the stove, on low heat.
4. Line a baking dish or storage container with parchment paper.
5. Form the batter into balls of even size and line them up on the parchment paper.
6. Use a spoon to scoop out some of the melted chocolate and drizzle it on each ball.
7. Place the balls in the fridge to allow the chocolate to set (around 30 minutes) before serving. Enjoy!

Use a mini-ice cream scoop to make the batter into even size balls.

DESSERT RECIPE 7
Chocolate Brownie Protein Ice Cream

PREP TIME: 10 MINUTES

COOK TIME: 0 MINUTES

READY IN: 10 MINUTES

SERVINGS: 1

MACROS WITHOUT TOPPINGS

CARBS 4g
PROTEIN 34g
FAT 4g
SUGAR 1g

CALORIES: 172

INGREDIENTS

- 5 EGG WHITES
- 1 SCOOP CHOCOLATE PROTEIN POWDER* (I prefer *Devotion* Brownie Batter Flavor).
- 2 TBS ALMOND MILK
- 2 CUPS ICE CUBES
- ¼ TSP SEA SALT
- ¼ TSP CINNAMON

TOPPINGS (OPTIONAL)**

- LOW CAL WHIP CREAM (I prefer *Redi Whip* Almond Flavor)
- 1 TBS SUGAR FREE CHOCOLATE CHIPS. (I prefer *LILY'S* brand).

NOTES: *If you have cut ice cream out of your diet because of the fat and calories, not to mention the bloating and gas from too much dairy (fun times). then this recipe is one you will be excited to try. This recipe is simple to make and produces a smooth and creamy dessert. It really has helped me satisfy my ice cream cravings in a much healthier way. It also is a great way to get in more protein for the day.*

*I use *Devotion* as my go to protein because it tastes great, contains whey protein isolate and micellar casein, plus digestive enzymes. You can find the link to *Devotion* on my website: Claremorrow.com under *My Favorites*. If you follow a vegan diet, you can experiment and try using a vegan protein to see how it turns out.

STEPS

1. Add to a blender the egg whites, one scoop of protein powder, almond milk, sea salt, and cinnamon (optional). Add in the ice cubes.
2. Turn the blender to medium high and blend all the ingredients for a few minutes until the mixture turns to a smooth and creamy ice cream.
3. Turn off the blender and pour the ice cream into a bowl and place in the freezer.
4. While the ice cream is chilling, place the Lily's chocolate chips in a bowl in the microwave or on the stove in a pan, and heat to melt the chips.
5. Remove the ice cream from the freezer. Pour the melted chocolate on top. Add a little bit (around two Tbs.) of the Lo Cal Whip Cream. Enjoy!

**With the toppings add; 40 calories, 4g carbs, 1g protein, 2g fat, 1g sugar.

DRINKS AND SMOOTHIES 1
Lo Cal Café Latte

PREP TIME: 5 MINUTES
COOK TIME: 5 MINUTES
READY IN: 10 MINUTES
SERVINGS: 1

HOT   ICED

	MACROS WITH WATER	WITH ALMOND MILK
	CARBS 1.5g	CARBS 2g
	PROTEIN 10g	PROTEIN 12g
	FAT 1.5g	FAT 4g
	SUGAR 0g	SUGAR 0g
CALORIES:	60	80

INGREDIENTS

- 16 OUNCES BREWED COFFEE (Makes one large café latte).
- ½ SCOOP PROTEIN POWDER (I prefer *Devotion* protein) *
- ½ CUP WATER OR ALMOND MILK (Unsweetened)
- CINNAMON

NOTES: *Drinking coffee daily while trying to lose fat is something I get asked about all the time. Coffee is fine to have when fat loss is a goal.* **The problem is all the sugar and cream most people add to their coffee.** *That's where the fat and calories start to add up! Black coffee is a great choice since it has zero fat and only five calories per cup. I like to have that before doing fasted cardio in the morning. With this recipe I can treat myself a few days per week with a latte because it is a healthier version and a good way to get in some extra protein for the day.*

* I use *Devotion* as my go to protein because it tastes great, contains whey protein isolate and micellar casein, plus digestive enzymes.

I use the Brownie Batter flavor to make a choco latte, and the Sinful Cinnamon Flavor for a vanilla cinnamon latte. Use any flavor of choice.

You can find the link to *Devotion* on my website: Claremorrow.com under *My Favorites*. If you follow a vegan diet, you can use a vegan protein for this recipe.

STEPS

1. Brew your favorite coffee. Non flavored coffee works best for this recipe.
2. Add ½ scoop protein powder into a tall cup.
3. Add in the ½ cup water or almond milk. Use an immersion blender to mix well until frothy.
4. Pour your coffee into a cup. If making iced latte, add in 4-5 ice cubes. Gently pour in the protein foam.
5. Stir gently with a tall spoon. Sprinkle cinnamon on top (optional). Enjoy!

DRINKS AND SMOOTHIES 2

Protein Pink Drink

PREP TIME: 5 MINUTES

COOK TIME: 0 MINUTES

READY IN: 5 MINUTES

SERVINGS: 1

MACROS

CARBS 5g
PROTEIN 11g
FAT 2g
SUGAR 3g

CALORIES: 80

INGREDIENTS

- 16 OZ ZERO CALORIE SPARKLING WATER/PINK OR RED NATURAL COLOR (I prefer *ICE brand* Black Raspberry flavor)
- ½ SCOOP PROTEIN POWDER (I prefer *Devotion* protein) *
- ½ CUP ALMOND MILK (Unsweetened).
- 3 RIPE STRAWBERRIES

NOTES Part of being successful with maintaining a healthy diet for life means learning how to be creative with healthy food swaps. During my Fluffy to Fit journey I found out when I denied myself of the tasty (but not so healthy) foods and drinks that I craved, I usually caved in after a few days and then I would binge eat. Then I would try to make up for it by over exercising the next day. Working with a bodybuilding coach helped me learn how to do food swaps like this recipe, so I could still enjoy some treats that satisfy cravings in a healthier way!

* I use *Devotion* as my go to protein because it tastes great, contains whey protein isolate and micellar casein, plus digestive enzymes.

I use the Angel Food Cake flavor for this recipe because it has a similar taste to vanilla.

You can find the link to *Devotion* on my website: Claremorrow.com under *My Favorites*. If you follow a vegan diet, you can use a vegan protein for this recipe.

STEPS

1. Wash the strawberries and cut them in half. Destem and set aside.
2. Fill a large glass halfway with ice cubes.
3. Pour the protein powder into a separate cup and add the ½ cup of almond milk and use an immersion blender until frothy.
4. Pour the sparkling soda over the ice.
5. Pour the protein milk blend over the soda.
6. Gently mix with a tall spoon or straw until blended.
7. Add your strawberries to the drink. Enjoy!

DRINKS AND SMOOTHIES 3

Very Berry Smoothie

PREP TIME: 10 MINUTES

COOK TIME: 0 MINUTES

READY IN: 10 MINUTES

SERVINGS: 1
MACROS
CARBS 17g
PROTEIN 5g
FAT 4g
SUGAR 11g

CALORIES: 116

INGREDIENTS

- 3 LARGE STRAWBERRIES
- ¼ CUP BLUEBERRIES
- ¼ CUP RASPBERRIES
- ½ CUP ALMOND MILK (Unsweetened)
- ¼ CUP GREEK YOGURT 0% (I prefer *FAGE'* brand).
- ½ CUP ICE

You can use frozen or fresh fruit for this recipe. If the fruit is frozen use less ice.

NOTES: *A question I get asked often is "Clare, should I skip meals and drink replacement shakes or smoothies instead?" My answer is "no." The best diet is one that consists of eating whole food. Not only is it more filling, but there are studies out there showing that chewing food helps release enzymes and hormones that help with digestion and feeling full.*

I do like smoothies and protein shakes for in between meals. *They come in handy for an on-the-go healthy snack and are a good way to get in some extra nutrients for the day. You can use any kind of berries you like in this recipe. I try to stick to berries for my fruit choice since some others like bananas or mango have more natural sugar and fat and that means more calories.*

OPTIONAL: Add in one scoop of protein powder. I use *Devotion* as my go to protein because it tastes great, contains whey protein isolate and micellar casein, plus digestive enzymes. You can find the link to *Devotion* on my website: Claremorrow.com under *My Favorites*. If you follow a vegan diet, you can use a vegan protein in this recipe. Make sure to adjust your macros.

STEPS

1. Rinse off the fruit, destem the strawberries and cut them in half.
2. In a blender, add the fruit, almond milk, yogurt, and blend. Add in the protein powder (if using) and blend again.
3. Slowly add in the ice. Blend until it's the consistency you like.
4. Garnish with a few blueberries or strawberries.

The key to making great smoothies (and ice cream) is to use a high-quality blender. The best blenders are more expensive but worth the investment. I have the blender I use listed on my *Amazon* page under my kitchen favorites list.

DRINKS AND SMOOTHIES 4

Low Calorie Mint Mojito Mocktail

PREP TIME: 5 MINUTES

COOK TIME: 0 MINUTES

READY IN: 5 MINUTES

SERVINGS: 1

MACROS
CARBS 5g
PROTEIN 2g
FAT 0g
SUGAR 2g

CALORIES: 20

INGREDIENTS

- 1 LARGE LIME
- 1 LARGE LEMON
- 1 CUP LOOSELY PACKED MINT LEAVES
- 12 OZ DIET LEMON SODA (i.e. *Sprite Zero* or Diet *7-Up*)
- ICE
- LIME OR LEMON SLICES FOR GARNISH

Mocktails are a great way to satisfy your "drink" cravings in a much healthier way. It may seem difficult to switch over, but the results you finally achieve with your fat loss goals will be worth it.

NOTES: *Because most alcoholic drinks are high in calories, I do not drink very much. When it comes to fat loss every calorie counts even the ones that are in liquid form. I would much rather get my calories from satiating foods rather than a drink that can be chug a lugged in 60 seconds. Not to mention one drink leads to just one more and then one more...and that never ends well. Lol!*

In addition to alcohol being high in calories, it is a toxin to our bodies. Because of that fat loss can come to a stop for 24-36 hours with just one or two drinks! *Instead of our body breaking down fats, it focuses on removing alcohol from our system as a priority. If you are having two or more alcoholic drinks per week and have hit a plateau with fat loss, especially belly fat, this could be why.*

STEPS

1. Gently rinse the mint leaves and allow them to dry.
2. In a large cup squeeze the juice from the lemon or lime (or a combo of both). You will want 1 ½ Tbs of juice total.
3. Use your fingers to tear up the mint leaves, allowing them to fall into the cup with the juice.
4. Use the back end of a dinner knife to mash the mint leaves. This allows the flavor of the mint to release.
5. Add your desired amount of ice into the cup. Pour in your lemon/lime soda.
6. Gently stir the mixture with a straw. A metal straw works best. Pierce the mint again with the end of the straw to release more flavor.
7. Let the drink stand for 1-2 minutes for the flavors to meld.
8. Serve with a straw and garnish the rim with lemon or lime slices. Enjoy!

If you need help getting started on your fitness journey, my first book *Fluffy to Fit* can be a great resource. *Fluffy to Fit* has 21 chapters such as, *How to Overcome Gym Shyness, How to Beat Sugar Cravings, What to Look for in a Gym, How to get Started Lifting, Hormone Balance and Fat Loss, Alcohol and Fat Loss,* and much more. The book talks about my background and how I made a career change from riding and training horses to competitive bodybuilder, all after the age of 40! *Fluffy to Fit* is a book for anyone of any age that needs more information on how to achieve success in their fitness journey. You can find *Fluffy to Fit* on *Amazon* in print and *Kindle*-or as an e book on my website, www.claremorrow.com

Scan the QR Code to Find the *Fluffy to Fit* Book

Manufactured by Amazon.ca
Bolton, ON

35683407R00057